Letters to
Pastors' Wives

Letters to
Pastors' Wives

BY

Meredith R. Sheppard
Foreword by Dr. Lois Evans

XULON PRESS

Xulon Press
2301 Lucien Way #415
Maitland, FL 32751
407.339.4217
www.xulonpress.com

Unless otherwise indicated, Scripture quotations taken from the King James Version (KJV) – *public domain.*

Scripture quotations taken from the Amplified Bible (AMP). Copyright © 1954, 1958, 1962, 1964, 1965, 1987 by The Lockman Foundation. Used by permission. All rights reserved.

Scripture quotations taken from The Message (MSG). Copyright © 1993, 1994, 1995, 1996, 2000, 2001, 2002. Used by permission of NavPress Publishing Group. Used by permission. All rights reserved.

Scripture quotations taken from the Holy Bible, New International Version (NIV). Copyright © 1973, 1978, 1984, 2011 by Biblica, Inc.™. Used by permission. All rights reserved.

Printed in the United States of America.

ISBN-13: 978-1-6305-0305-5

Dedication

This book is dedicated to the memory of my mother
Frances Perkins Richardson who, along with my father,
raised me in the fear and admonition of the Lord.

And to my mother-in-love Peggy Sheppard,
a pastor's wife for over 45 years. By her life
she showed me how to love my husband and family
and how to love and serve God and His people.

Table of Contents

Foreword

W hen I think of my dear friend Meredith, I always think of how God brought us together, "For such a time as this." (Esther 4:14)

We met over lunch in Hawaii at a conference where our husbands were speakers. As we ate and fellowshipped, I found out that Meredith was a fellow Pastor's Wife. I immediately leaned in to share with Meredith that the Lord had placed on my heart the need to start a conference for Pastor's Wives.

Meredith told me to let her know when I planned the mini-pilot conference and she would be there. She also shared that she had a ministry and a newsletter called *Wives In Touch*. We exchanged contact information and I began receiving empowering and encouraging ministry newsletters from Meredith.

Having received confirmation that the event on my heart was indeed needed, I proceeded to plan my first conference for Pastors' Wives in 1999. On the day of the event, to my surprise, Meredith was present and she has been present in my life and as a ministry partner ever since.

Over the years, I realized I met a calm, cool, collected woman, but give her the Word of God and you will experience a powerful, passionate, dynamic, gifted Bible Teacher and lover of God's Word. She leads you directly into deep, spiritual, practical truth on stage and during personal times.

What Meredith and I have in common is our shared passion for Pastors' Wives. Pastors' Wives are often the unsung heroes of church ministry. We have to support our husbands, use our gifts to support the ministry, demonstrate hospitality, keep up with kids, and all the while share the burdens that naturally come with church ministry. And yes, all of this is expected to be done with a smile.

That is why this book by my good friend is so timely. She offers a helpful, healing touch that will strengthen, encourage and inspire Pastors' Wives as they continue to fulfill the high calling God has placed on their lives.

This fine work will let these special ladies know they are not alone on their journey. On the contrary, they are a part of an elite group of women who have been uniquely created and gifted to make a special, one of a kind contribution to His Kingdom and for His Glory.

Lois Evans

Preface

The selection of letters contained in this book were originally known as Wives In Touch, a ministry of prayer and encouragement for pastors' wives. It has always been my desire to share honestly and openly about the joys and challenges we experience. *"If one part suffers, every part suffers with it; if one part is honored, every part rejoices with it"* (1 Corinthians 12:26).

For years I pondered and prayed about putting my thoughts into letter format. That plan was realized in 1993. Before blogs, Facebook, or Twitter, I began mailing these letters to the pastors' wives I knew. And somewhat like the old Faberge shampoo commercial, "I told two friends and they told two friends, and so on and so on and so on." Sixteen years later hundreds of pastors' wives were receiving and still requesting Wives In Touch.

With every letter sent, my prayer was that each recipient would know that she was not alone. Neither are you! As pastors' wives we can weep and rejoice together. As you read this book may you be affirmed, informed, and encouraged. There really can be companionship in the calling and joy for the journey. God bless you.

His love and mine,
Meredith

At First Glance

1

The Journey Begins

I t is hard to believe that so much time has passed, but March 1989 is unforgettable. That is when my pastor/ husband Paul and I, along with our young daughter, younger son, and all of our worldly possessions, moved from Pennsylvania to California. Paul was following the Lord's leading to shepherd a flock on the west coast. He obeyed the call to, *"... Be not afraid, but speak, and hold not thy peace: For I am with thee, and no man shall set on thee to hurt thee: for I have much people in this city"* (Acts 18:9-10 KJV).

I followed my husband, armed with the sentiment Ruth expressed to Naomi. *"Whither thou goest, I will go; and whither thou lodgest, I will lodge: thy people shall be my people, and thy God my God"* (Ruth 1:16 KJV).

Those early days are treasured memories. I fell quickly and deeply, head-over-heels in love with California. The state's natural beauty is breathtaking—palm trees, fruit trees, scenic coasts, majestic mountains, the Pacific Ocean, and the rich diversity of people.

As God challenged us, Paul challenged the congregation. We were being stretched and so were the people. This body of believers grasped God's vision for the church and submitted to the leadership of the young pastor from back East.

After a while, however, I began to realize the perimeters and limitations imposed upon relationships when you are "the pastor's wife." Where other women are able to share freely about challenges or hardships related to their husband's job, I could not. Suddenly innocuous incidents occurring within our home became choice morsels to be shared among those hungry for the inside scoop. Some women sought a relationship with me because I was the pastor's wife, while others avoided me for the same reason.

Being new to the state and a homemaker, the only women I knew were from our congregation. A general feeling of isolation began to envelop me. In so many ways I was just like my sisters at church, but in other ways I was distinctly different. Without being married to a pastor, how could any other woman in the church know how I felt?

One particular day I cried out to the Lord in desperation. "No other woman in the church knows how I feel. I don't have any real friends. Why can't I ever share personal requests for prayer without it being misinterpreted as trouble in my marriage or that the pastor is about to resign?" I felt all alone and threw plenty of pity parties. The truth is, being the wife of a pastor does make you a bit different!

Our gracious God reminded me of various pastors' wives I knew. Alma knows how you feel. Kris knows how you feel. Bobbi can relate to what you're experiencing. With a rising sense of connectedness my spirits rose also. There are women the world over who are married to ministers and who think and feel the way I do. Thinking of them took my mind off of me. Strengthened in the knowledge of their existence prompted me to pray for them. For the next few years, especially when I was tempted to think, 'Nobody knows the trouble I've seen,' I would pray for pastors' wives. Praying for you, your families, and ministries is a blessing and privilege. As I experience the joys and challenges of ministry life, I know I am not alone, and neither are you.

Andrae Crouch wrote a song that says, "Somebody somewhere is praying, just for you. They may not know your name, but they're praying just the same. Somebody, somewhere is praying just for you."[1]

The very first time I heard that song I thought of precious pastors' wives and lifted you up in prayer. I still do.

2

Leaving, Lodging, and Loving

I n a remarkable display of love and loyalty a young widow named Ruth, with little more than the clothes on her back, leaves everything and everyone that is familiar in order to accompany her also widowed mother-in-law to Bethlehem. The words Ruth utters convey such deep devotion and commitment that today many couples use the same words in their marriage ceremonies.

> *"Entreat me not to leave you, or turn back from following you. **For wherever you go, I will go; and wherever you lodge, I will lodge. Your people shall be my people, and your God, my God.** Where you die, I will die, and there will I be buried. The Lord do*

*so to me, and more also, if anything but death parts
you and me"* (Ruth 1:16-17 NKJV).

Ruth's allegiance and unwavering fidelity was not just to her mother-in-law Naomi, but also to Naomi's God. Ruth may not have known what the future held but she trusted in a God who held her future. There are some invaluable insights pastors' wives can glean from Ruth's story.

"Wherever you go, I will go." Following God often requires relocating.

Countless pastors' wives lament leaving homes, family, friends, churches, etc., when their husbands are called to serve elsewhere. They go, but sometimes grudgingly. A songwriter penned the words, "The safest place in the whole wide world is in the will of God." Ruth willingly and whole-heartedly left her hometown of Moab and clung not only to Naomi but also to a faithful God.

*"The Lord God said, "It is not good for the man
to be alone. I will make a helper suitable for him"*
(Genesis 2:18).

*"Therefore shall a man leave his father and his mother,
and shall cleave unto his wife: and they shall be one flesh"*
(Genesis 2:24 KJV).

> *"I tell you the truth," Jesus replied, "no one who has left home or brothers or sisters or mother or father or children or fields for me and the gospel will fail to receive a hundred times as much in this present age (homes, brothers, sisters, mothers, children and fields—and with them persecutions) and in the age to come, eternal life"* (Mark 10:29-30).

"Wherever you lodge I will lodge." When the Prince of Peace abides within we can make our abode anywhere.

The Hebrew word for lodge has two meanings. One definition means to stop overnight; to dwell in temporarily; to reside or to stay permanently. Another definition is used negatively and means to become obstinate especially in words, to complain, murmur.

Attitude has more to do with the beauty, comfort, and contentment of a dwelling place than interior design, fine food, or furnishings. The book of Proverbs underscores this truth. *"Better a little with the fear of the Lord than great wealth with turmoil. Better a meal of vegetables where there is love than a fattened calf with hatred. Better a dry crust with peace and quiet than a house full of feasting with strife. Better to live on a corner of the roof than share a house with a quarrelsome wife"* (Proverbs 15:16-17, 17:1, 21:9, 25:24).

"Your people shall be my people, and your God my God." Pastors' wives, we love God by loving His people.

The congregation is not just your husband's people. You must accept, love, and embrace them as your people as well.

In their book *Every Woman in the Bible*, Sue and Larry Richards write: "The order in which Ruth expressed her commitment is significant. In Old Testament times Israel alone had a covenant relationship with God. Ruth, aware of this relationship, pledged that "your people shall be my people," fully aware that in committing herself to God's covenant community she was also committing herself to Israel's God."[2]

> *"God is not unjust; he will not forget your work and the love you have shown him as you have helped his people and continue to help them"* (Hebrews 6:10).

> *"The King will reply, "I tell you the truth, whatever you did for one of the least of these brothers of mine, you did for me"* (Matthew 25:40).

I encourage you to read the book of Ruth for a beautiful refresher course in leaving, lodging, and loving God and His people.

Where He leads me, I will follow... I'll go with Him, with Him all the way.[3]

3

Basic Training

W e assume quite a demanding role and yet pastors' wives continue to be the most untrained of all Christian professionals. In the book *Heart To Heart With Pastors' Wives* contributing author Mary Lou Whitlock writes, "Many wives pleaded for help with ministry skills and wished they had been the recipients of more help and advance preparation before they were launched into varying degrees of leadership roles."[4] (Based on the *NAE survey results.)

Whitlock goes on to say, "We must arm ourselves with truth and wisdom to do God's work in a fallen world... Seminary training for women should be an encouragement to run the race with joy and enthusiasm, using the time we have wisely..."

Growing numbers of Bible colleges and seminaries are hearing and heeding our plea. Courses are now offered just for pastors' wives—Ministry Preparation for Partners. Some of the topics taught include: Old and New Testament surveys, Bible study methods, Bible doctrine, women in leadership, basic counseling skills, how to share your faith, personal evangelism, personal/family finance, parenting skills, physical fitness, hospitality, temperament/personality, effective relationships, speech made easy, communication, and developing a women's ministry. It's wonderful to know these kinds of courses are now being offered. At some institutions they are cost-free if the spouse is enrolled as a full-time student.

As wonderful as this is, for many going to school is simply not feasible. I would venture to say that most pastors' wives do *not* attend seminary, even if college educated. Therefore what are we to do? I believe the answer is home schooling and on-the-job training. We can become students of the Word even if we never attend seminary or Bible college.

Early in our marriage a wise minister, who has since gone home to be with the Lord, spoke these words to me. "Let God prepare you... Be spiritual. Stay in the Word. In Paul's ministry he will need a spiritual wife, not one who is slothful. You must be spiritual. Prepare to be a first lady. Stay in the Word. Be spiritual..."

Those words, written in a journal and dated September 21, 1984, are just as encouraging today as when they were first spoken. All believers are chosen by God, gifted by God, to be used in service to God. Therefore we must lean heavily upon Him, the living Word, to prepare us. The apostle Paul wrote a letter of encouragement to a young Timothy saying, *"You have known the holy Scriptures, which are able to make you wise for salvation through faith in Christ Jesus. All Scripture is God-breathed and is useful for teaching, rebuking, correcting and training in righteousness, so that the man of God may be thoroughly equipped for every good work"* (2 Timothy 3:15-16).

The wise and challenging advice Paul gave to Timothy holds true for pastors' wives, as well. If you feel ill equipped as a pastor's wife—get into the Word! The Word transforms while renewing the mind. The Word teaches, rebukes, corrects, and trains in righteousness so that we are fully equipped for every good work...even the work of the pastor's wife.

Becoming students of the Word and living a life of prayer, I believe, is the basic training and best preparation for being successful at the work of the pastor's wife. E. Stanley Jones wrote this about prayer:

Prayer is cooperation with God. In prayer you align your desires, your will and your life to God. You and God become agreed on life desires, life purposes, life plans and you work them out together. Prayer, then, is not trying to get God to do our will. It is the getting of our will into line with God's will. So prayer aligns the whole self to the whole Self of God. Prayer is therefore attunement. Just as when a note on a well-turned piano is struck, the corresponding note on a well-tuned violin will vibrate in unison, so when God strikes certain notes in His nature, we find our heart-strings vibrating in unison, provided prayer has attuned us.

...Prayer cleanses, it chastens our desires, realigns them so that you cannot tell where your desires end and God's desires begin. They are one. The desires are one, the decisions are one, and the power is one... When you learn how to pray, you learn how to live—vitally, vibrantly, victoriously.[5]

"Let God prepare you. Stay in the Word. Be spiritual."

4

Designer's Original

Various identifying tags come attached to new garments—size, price, designer's name or logo, small envelope with spare buttons, etc. One day while removing these tags from a newly purchased outfit, I paid particular attention to one that read: *The irregularities and variations in the color and texture of this fabric are characteristic of the fabric adding to its natural beauty and is in no way to be considered as defective.*

How accepting I am of the simple wording written on that tag. What may be viewed initially as snags, catches, or flaws in the fabric, are simply slubs. Slubs are those slight irregularities produced purposely by knotting, twisting, or using uneven lengths of fiber when spinning or manufacturing. This accounts for the slight variations in seemingly identical garments.

Oh that people, women especially, would come to accept themselves and one another with such sweet and liberating simplicity. It can be a real struggle resisting the relentless urge to compare oneself to another, regarding appearance or ability. When we should understand our uniqueness and accept our attributes, we often despise our differences. Christians are not exempt, neither are pastors' wives.

"Pastor's Wife" is a title without a job description. Therefore the tendency to pattern ourselves after pastors' wives we know and/or admire is great. Betty J. Coble in her book *The Private Life of the Minister's Wife* writes, "Learn from her. Do not compare yourself with her... What we should look to others for is encouragement, not comparison... Accepting yourself as you are and liking what God has given you to work with gives you a very necessary tool for building a better relationship with God and with others."[6]

I am a far cry from the stereotypical pastor's wife. I do not wear hats, play the piano, sing in the choir, or work in the children's ministry. But one thing I am competent and confident at is being myself!

Being yourself takes courage. It also honors God.

"So God created man in His own image, in the image of God He created him; male and female He created them" (Genesis 1:27).

"I praise you because I am fearfully and wonderfully made; your works are wonderful; I know that full well" (Psalm 139:14).

The word fearfully means reverently, with honor, esteem, respect tinged with awe. Wonderfully means to distinguish, put a difference, show marvelous, separate, set apart.

God uses Himself as the pattern of perfection for our lives. However we do not all look alike. By God's own design we have differing strengths, abilities, giftings, and personalities. Coble goes on to say, "In order to know what qualities you have for use in ministering to others, it is necessary for you to be acquainted with yourself and your worth before God."

God desires to use you. If unsure of who you are and of God's plans and purposes for your life, pray! Expect God to answer. Read the Bible and expect God to reveal who He created you to be. It is in Him that we live, move, and have our being.

The late Danniebelle Hall wrote and recorded the song Designer's Original. The chorus says:

Designer's Original

You're a Designer's Original
You're one of a kind
Created by the Master, with one purpose in mind
To be a showcase of His glory, for the whole world to see;
A reflection of His beauty, as it shines through you and me.[7]

You were created an original. Don't live your life as a copy!

5

Hide-and-Seek

W hen I was a little girl, on any given day you could hear the familiar shout, "Come out, come out, wherever you are!" The one shouting was "It" and the call was to hidden playmates. Once discovered, they had to run to a designated spot called base and touch it before the caller could tag them. The person who got tagged before reaching base became the new "It." He or she would close their eyes and count, giving the others a chance to hide. The game would continue on and on—until we tired of playing, our parents called us inside, or it got too dark to play safely. Every once in a while a game ended in frustration and hurt feelings when the one who was It failed to find those who were too well hidden.

It may surprise you to know how often I think of Hide-and-Seek, not the game many of us played as children but the one many pastors' wives find themselves engaged in.

18

The following is a brief excerpt from the book, *Help! I'm a Pastor's Wife*.

"I am reminded of the two little boys with the terrible "aging disease," one from South Africa and the other from the United States. When they met for the first time at Disneyland several years ago, they looked at one another with amazement. After years of wondering if there was anyone else like them anywhere, they had found each other. I understand they became friends immediately."

Obviously, there is a multitude of pastors' wives somewhere. But the big question is, how do we find one another?

Before we answer that question, let me ask another—Why do we hide? The answers, although varied, are common. People put us on pedestals because of who our husband is. We experience the betrayal of confidences. Somehow what we thought was a necessary protective shell became an impenetrable barrier. The walls of the glass house cave in on us. We continually face the unreal expectations of what and/or how a pastor's wife ought to be. At some point we have all had to wrestle with fears, insecurities, loneliness, hurts, misunderstandings, etc. Those who tire of the unrelenting struggle simply go into hiding. While others who feel like "It" cry, "Come out, come out wherever you are!" How do we find each other?

Even as children, it was usually more fun hiding than seeking. Being "It" meant searching and working alone although surrounded by unseen friends. So it is with pastors' wives. Many are hidden behind busy schedules and smiling masks, silently longing to have true fellowship and communion with those desperately seeking their company and companionship. Who are you in the game of Hide-and-Seek?

Finding one another requires faith—-in God and one another. With a little personal revision, Ecclesiastes 4:9 and 12 says, *"Two [pastors' wives] are better than one, because they have a good return for their work: If one falls down, her friend can help her up. But pity the [pastor's wife] who falls and has no one to help her up! Though one may be overpowered, two can defend themselves. A cord of three strands is not quickly broken."*

To those in hiding, heed the call—Come out, come out, wherever you are! We're all in this "game" together. *"Now the body is not made up of one part but many. If one part suffers, every part suffers with it; if one part is honored, every part rejoices with it"* (1 Corinthians 12:14, 26).

To those who are seeking, be encouraged! *"Ask and it will be given to you; seek and you will find; knock and the door will be opened to you. For everyone who asks receives; [s]he who seeks finds..."* (Matthew 7:7-8).

Another game we played as children was Follow the Leader. Finding one another requires faith to follow the Leader. As believers, the Holy Spirit leads and guides us.

Without faith Wives In Touch would have always been a dream and never a reality. It required faith to act upon the leading of the Holy Spirit, to go beyond thinking about and praying for pastors' wives to actually writing them. So many times the enemy would hiss and whisper, "Who do you think wants to read your silly little letters? What makes you think anyone even wants it?" However, by faith the first issue of Wives In Touch was mailed in October 1993 and continued to reach pastors' wives around the world for the next 16 years.

Is God leading you to reach out to another pastor's wife, to start or attend a fellowship or support group for pastors' wives, to pray for or with a pastor's wife? Follow the Leader. *"... Faith by itself, if it is not accompanied by action, is dead"* (James 2:17).

Many years ago I met Jean Coleman, a precious pastor's wife from Laurel, Maryland. Years before she and her husband Jack became heavily involved in missions, Jean published The Pastor's Helpmate, a monthly newsletter for pastors' wives. After receiving copies of Wives In Touch Jean wrote me and said, "It is obvious that the Lord has given us both the same vision for pastors' wives, and I rejoice that we can be co-laborers together to this vast field of lonely and hurting women. Did you know that there are nearly 300,000 pastors' wives in the United States? We both need to pray for many more to be drawn into this outreach ministry. Our sisters are crying out for a friend! May we be the answer to their prayers."

You may be the answer to the prayers of a fellow pastor's wife. It takes one to know one. We are our own best resource!

Finally, encourage one another. A little encouragement goes a long way, especially for that one who may be growing weary. *"Therefore, as we have opportunity, let us do good to all people, especially to those who belong to the family of believers"* (Galatians 6:9-10).

Step out in faith to find one another. Step out in faith to follow the Leader. Step out in faith to fulfill what God has placed on your heart!

Prayer

Father help me to take my eyes off of myself. Who needs a word of encouragement, a card, a prayer, a hug, a smile, etc.? By faith, I will reach out to her. Amen

6

Models Wanted

Have you ever considered a career in modeling? What's your idea of a model? The dictionary defines model as: a thing or person to be imitated; a standard for imitation; worthy to serve as a model; exemplary; to carry oneself in such a way as to call forth imitation in others.

With that as our working definition, I think you'll agree that as pastors' wives we've been called into modeling. In many different ways our manner of behavior influences others. Without intending to, we can and do cause others to imitate us.

One Sunday my hairstylist asked me if I'd noticed how many women in the church had gotten their hair cut after I had mine cut. I hadn't noticed and certainly didn't think it had anything to do with me. However I do recall the response of a friend's husband when she got her hair cut,

"It looks like Meredith's." Modeling a hairstyle is one thing but modeling a lifestyle is quite another.

Shortly after my husband began pastoring, I received a new modeling assignment. Submission! Paul would agree that I am a submitted and loving wife but I did not always submit to him as my pastor.

On one occasion when we needed workers for a newly formed children's ministry, my husband asked me to fill in until others could be recruited and trained. If he had only been my pastor I would have most certainly complied with his request. But as his wife I felt entirely comfortable and justified in saying, "You've got to be kidding. I don't want to teach Sunday school or work in children's church. Have you seen the behavior of some of those kids? Give me a break."

Even now I have trouble believing I said those things and meant them. If Paul ever told me that any other member of the church was that uncooperative or difficult to work with I'd be shocked and saddened.

As pastors' wives we know the heartaches and disappointments of the shepherd perhaps better than anyone else. When sheep buck and balk at loving leadership our hearts ache, too. Why then did I fail to see it in myself? Paul saw my abilities and talents lying dormant within me. I only saw rambunctious kids who wouldn't sit still.

One day during my devotions the Lord asked me, "How would My church be if every member submitted to leadership by following your example? How can your husband have full confidence in you when you murmur and complain about so many things?" Convicted by the realization of grieving my shepherds, I quickly repented.

Since that time I've been encouraged and motivated by the following Scriptures. *"(Pastors') Wives, submit to your husbands as to the Lord. For the husband is the head of the wife as Christ is the head of the church, his body, of which he is the Savior. Now as the church submits to Christ, so also should (pastors') wives submit to their husbands in everything"* (Ephesians 5:22-24 NIV). *"Obey your leaders and submit to their authority. They keep watch over you as men who must give an account. Obey them so that their work will be a joy, not a burden, for that would be of no advantage to you"* (Hebrews 13:17 NIV).

Modeling may not always seem glamorous. The work is demanding and the hours long, but the pay and benefits are eternal.

7

Setting the Standard

A Morning Prayer

Heavenly Father, this is the day that You have made. I will rejoice and be glad in it. So far today no corrupt communication has come from my mouth. My thoughts and affections have been on things above and not on things below. It has been a glorious and victorious day thus far, and I give you all the praise! But in a moment I am going to have to get out of bed and I earnestly plead for Your help! Amen

Ninety minutes after getting out of bed I find myself standing outside the church talking to a co-worker about another member of our church's staff. We discuss the frustration of working on a team with a "Lone Ranger-type," who tends to interpret teamwork as everyone doing things her way. Immediately I sense the Lord's displeasure. The woman I'm talking to tries in vain to encourage me by saying, "Everyone needs to vent, even pastors' wives." Acknowledging the truth in her statement I agree, "Yes, everyone needs to vent from time to time. However this time God is telling me that venting is done best in His presence, and in prayer." My response sobers her. Rather reluctantly she agrees, "I know that's true. But it just feels so much better to vent with my girlfriend."

Venting with a girlfriend may feel satisfying, but it rarely solves a problem. If the truth be told, most times we are not seeking solutions when we vent. We want to let off some steam. God did not tell me that venting is wrong. He just told me to come to Him with my frustrations. Why? He wants me to model His grace, albeit under fire, before my co-workers.

I used to think that was unfair, but not anymore. It delights me to know that God loves me so much and wants to make me more like Him. *My [daughter], do not make light of the Lord's discipline, and do not lose heart when he rebukes you, because the Lord disciplines those he loves, and he punishes everyone he accepts as a [daughter]. God disciplines us for our good, that we may share in his holiness"* (Hebrews 12:5-6, 10b).

As pastors' wives we are in a prime position to influence others by our conduct, positively or negatively. Queen Vashti was a woman in a prominent position. Her public refusal to honor her husband's unreasonable request struck fear in the hearts of the king's men.

> *"According to law, what must be done to Queen Vashti? She has not obeyed the command of King Xerxes that the eunuchs have taken to her. Queen Vashti has done wrong, not only against the king but also against all the nobles and the peoples of all the provinces of King Xerxes. For the queen's conduct will become known to all the women, and so they will despise their husbands and say, 'King Xerxes commanded Queen Vashti to be brought before him, but she would not come.' This very day the Persian and Median women of the nobility who have heard about the queen's conduct will respond to all the king's nobles in the same way. There will be no end of disrespect and discord"*
> (Esther 1:15-18).

Little did Queen Vashti suspect would be the long-range consequences of her conduct. She was deposed as queen, banished forever from the king's presence, and never mentioned again in the pages of Scripture.

Whenever I read Queen Vashti's story I think of pastors' wives. We have the ability to influence others by our conduct. Had I not allowed the Holy Spirit to silence me that day outside the church, venting may have given way to gossip. A few days after that incident the co-worker I talked to said, "I've made up a new rule: Only good news! I'm not talking negatively about anybody, even if it's true." By praying about the situation we have come to see our hearts changing, the atmosphere at work brighten, and the employee in question working hard at getting along better with the rest of the staff.

> *"[She] who heeds discipline shows the way to life, but whoever ignores correction leads others astray"* (Proverbs 10:17).

Showing the way to life is not always easy. Neither is: living in a glass house, constantly being placed upon a pedestal, having our lives scrutinized, etc. However, God does not require of pastors' wives what is not required of all believers. We just happen to be more visible. Like it or not, how we live our lives has bearing on the lives of countless others. The sooner we understand this fact, the better off we will be. Pastor's wife, God loves you. We are His daughters. The King of Kings is our Father. We are a chosen people, a royal priesthood, a holy nation, a people belonging to God, that we may declare the praises of Him who called us out of darkness into His wonderful light.

God longs to purify, polish, and prepare us for His service. This is often accomplished through heated trials. God uses trials to rid our lives of dross in much the same way we visit the spa. Massage refreshes the body and soul, softening muscles and soothing nerves. It also releases everyday stress while facilitating freedom of movement. *"I beat my body and make it my slave so that after I have preached to others, I myself will not be disqualified for the prize"* (1 Corinthians 9:27).

We endure intense heat so that toxins and impurities are eliminated from our bodies. *"This third I will bring into the fire; I will refine them like silver and test them like gold. They will call on my name and I will answer them; I will say, 'They are my people,' and they will say, 'The Lord is our God'"* (Zechariah 13:9).

We willingly submit ourselves to the discomfort of "beauty treatments." European facials are wonderful, but the extraction process can be downright excruciating. And what about mud treatments? Having mud applied gently with a brush or experiencing a mud bath feels a whole lot different from the unkind, untrue accusations of mud-slinging. However, enduring it well has the same result.

> *"No discipline seems pleasant at the time, but painful. Later on, however, it produces a harvest of righteousness and peace for those who have been trained by it. Therefore, strengthen your feeble arms and weak knees. Make level paths for your feet, so that*

the lame may not be disabled, but rather healed"
(Hebrews 12:11-13).

Finally, *"Consider it pure joy, my [sisters], whenever you face trials of many kinds, because you know
that the testing of your faith develops perseverance.
Perseverance must finish its work so that you may be
mature and complete, not lacking anything. Blessed is
the [pastor's wife] who perseveres under trial, because
when [she] has stood the test, [she] will receive the
crown of life that God has promised to those who love
him"* (James 1:2-4, 12).

8

Living Under a Microscope

Years ago, I cut out a newspaper cartoon showing a scene from a therapist's office. The therapist is an amoeba and the patient lying on a couch is a paramecium. The caption reads, "Well, I just feel like I'm living under a microscope."

Granted, as a schoolgirl I really liked science classes, hence my affinity for this cartoon. Nevertheless, as pastors' wives I'm sure many of you have had the feeling of living under a microscope. I certainly have. First ladies from the preacher's wife to the president's wife have always captured the attention of others. Scrutiny comes with the territory.

One pastor's wife expressed her surprise over a rumor circulating within her congregation. Because she had not worn nail polish for several weeks, people began saying her husband forbid her to do so. In amazement she exclaimed, "You mean people watch you down to your fingernails?!"

Many expectations accompany the role of pastor's wife, our own and those of others. However, we must strive to live up to God's expectations, which are always realistic and doable through the enabling power of the Holy Spirit.

After my husband began pastoring, my prayer was simply, "Lord, make me *me*. Whoever you created me to be, that is who I want to be." Why waste time trying to be someone I am not or doing things for which I am neither gifted nor talented?

Self-acceptance is a major key to experiencing joy and fulfillment as a pastor's wife. When you are comfortable with who you are and how God uses you, the expectations of others will mean less and less.

Being closely observed is inevitable but it does not have to be negative. By the grace of God we can say like the early apostles, *"We too are only [women] human like you"* (Acts 14:15a).

Upon Closer Inspection

9

This Little Light of Mine

W ho is the pastor's wife? Where is the pastor's wife? *You're* the pastor's wife?! These and other questions are asked repeatedly in many churches. Curiosity and sometimes envy cloaks the woman who ministers alongside and supports the man of God. Ours is a unique position that comes with a great deal of popularity—the byproduct of marrying a minister.

The title "First Lady" conjures up different images for different people—paragon of virtue, gracious hostess, and status symbol, just to name a few. Pastors' wives are widely recognized, frequently criticized, and often emulated.

No doubt the same kind of curiosity and speculation swirled around the women in Jesus' life. What was it about Mary and her sister Martha that drew Jesus to their home? As Mary sat at his feet what did they say to one another?

What was Martha's menu as she busily prepared a meal for the Master?

I once heard a minister say, "There's always a story behind the glory." I think of that saying when I read Luke 8:1-3. *"Jesus traveled about from one town and village to another, proclaiming the good news of the kingdom of God. The Twelve were with him, **and also some women** who had been cured of evil spirits and diseases: Mary (called Magdalene) from whom seven demons had come out; Joanna the wife of Cuza, the manager of Herod's household; Susanna; and many others. These women were helping to support them out of their own means."*

Despite their differing backgrounds these women possessed resources that enabled them to support the man of God. People must have wondered how they came to be in the glorious company of Jesus.

In light of her past, how valuable Mary Magdalene must have been in understanding the need for ministering deliverance to those suffering from demonic oppression. Perhaps Joanna knew how to relate to the upper class who were feeling down-and-out. And how much more can one sympathize with the sick and afflicted when they themselves have known healing and the Healer?

Our present status is due to our past experiences, the story behind the "glory." That which is painful, sinful, or shameful is worked together for good when we give it to God. As our past is processed properly, our resources are enriched.

For me, the limelight of being the pastor's wife is something over which I must be a good steward. As others look at me, my prayer is that they see Jesus. However I'd be less than honest if I said I never felt pressured by public scrutiny. There are certain times when I would appreciate the anonymity of being just another woman in the church.

In 1993 I was devastated by the sudden and shocking death of my sister. At the time I was working, going to school, and our family was in the process of moving to a new home. After my sister's death, Paul and I became the legal guardians of her teenaged daughter. One month after our niece moved in with us, my father died. I felt like I would never recover from each new set of circumstances. Although being in the limelight exacerbated the grief and stress I experienced, it also served to make others aware of my need for prayer and support.

Others may see our tears and trials but they also see our triumphs. As we "endure hardness as good soldiers" many are encouraged by our example.

We may be known for whose wife we are but we will be rewarded for whose servant we are.

"Let your [lime]light so shine before men, that they may see your good works and glorify your Father which is in heaven"   (Matthew 5:16 NKJV).

10

Lady Liberty

Ellis Island in New York Harbor was the gateway to America for more than 12 million immigrants between 1892 and 1924. The Statue of Liberty was the first structure many immigrants saw as they entered the country. It became a world symbol of the United States as a place of freedom, refuge, and hope.

The statue portrays liberty in the form of a woman. She wears flowing robes. Her head is adorned with a seven-spiked crown symbolizing the seven seas and seven continents. Lady Liberty bears a torch in her right hand and in her left, a book of law. Broken chains, symbolizing the overthrow of tyranny, lie at her feet.

Words of welcome penned by Emma Lazarus are indelibly inscribed at the base of the statue.

"... Give me your tired, your poor.
Your huddled masses yearning to breathe free.

The wretched refuse of your teeming shore.
Send these, the homeless, tempest-tost to me.
I lift my lamp beside the golden door!"

In a very real sense—those who flee oppression, poverty, persecution, injustice, those who are foreigners and aliens, the disenfranchised, those who are weary and in need of rest, the poor and needy, the huddled masses of society who yearn for the freedom found only in God's Son, the wretched, homeless, and solitary people seeking that sense of true belonging and family, and those who have been battered and beaten, tempest-tossed by the storms of life—those who seek a place of refuge and hope come from all over the world bringing their baggage and arrive at the doors of the Church.

Upon arriving in America immigrants found hope in Lady Liberty. As people come to our churches, do you, first lady, display the hope they seek?

Much like Lady Liberty, pastors' wives who yield to the transforming power of the Holy Spirit symbolize the liberating power of Christ (John 8:36). God clothes us with strength and dignity (Proverbs 31:25), garments of salvation and robes of righteousness (Isaiah 61:10). Upon our head is a crown of God's beauty (Isaiah 61:3). As bearers of His light we shine for the entire world to see our good deeds and praise our Heavenly Father (Matthew 5:14, 16).

First ladies who open their hearts to the Lord can then open their arms to the poor and extend their hands to the needy (Proverbs 31:8-9, 20). In this way we honor God (Proverbs 14:21).

And yet, we often tire and grow weary in well doing. Some of you first ladies reading this may be presently experiencing such fatigue. Over time, even Lady Liberty began to show signs of wear. Beginning in 1984, she underwent two years of extensive renovations. A team of French and American craftsmen repaired popped rivets, replaced corroded iron ribs, and strengthened her arm that had been incorrectly installed 100 years earlier. Even the old flame was replaced.

Popped rivets, corroded ribs, weak arms...have you ever felt this way? I know I have. How good to know that God is committed to our continual renewal. Spending time in His presence is "the pause that refreshes." Feeble hands are strengthened and weak knees made steady. When our hearts are overwhelmed (corroded ribs?) we can run to the Rock that is higher than I and find refuge (Psalm 61:1-4). As we look unto God we are enlightened and become the reflection of his glory.

"Come to me, all you who are weary and burdened, and I will give you rest. Take my yoke upon you and learn from me, for I am gentle and humble

in heart, and you will find rest for your souls"
(Matthew 11:28-29). The book of Mark records
five separate occasions when Jesus took His disciples away to a quiet place to escape the crush of
the crowd and find rest. God promises rest for the
weary. He continues to lead beside still waters and
restore our souls.

As we reflect upon Lady Liberty may she remind us
that our influence is lasting and eternal. This world will only
find true freedom, refuge, and hope—in Christ Jesus. As
we experience His rest and restoration we can point the
way. May the light of the Lord shine brightly through you
to those who make their way to the doors of your church.

11

Dare To Go Bare

Years ago a friend told me about a terrific store that sells designer clothes at a fraction of retail cost. Although the store's location was a bit out of the way she promised me it was worth the drive. Sure enough, it was. Intoxicated by so many affordable selections, I virtually staggered to the fitting room clutching an armload of clothes. However, once through the curtained doorway I immediately sobered. The room had no stalls, partitions, or privacy, just one huge mirrored room with long wooden benches bordering the four walls and women of various shapes and sizes in various stages of undress.

Vivid images of my own "least comely parts" flashed before my eyes—stretch marks, surgical scars, skin and undergarments with failing elasticity. I was faced with a dilemma. How badly do I want this? How much of myself do I dare expose? These are also questions pastors' wives ask themselves regarding relationships. How much can I risk exposing?

From the beginning of time when Eve chose fig leaves to cover herself, women have been hiding behind one thing or another: cosmetics and prosthetics, hair we dye and some we buy, collagen for fuller lips and liposuction for slimmer hips, silicone implants to enhance the bust and for the less daring Wonder-bras are a must. On a daily basis we carefully clothe, conceal, and camouflage that which we do not want others to see. Yet on the inside, pastors' wives are crying out to be known, loved, and accepted, warts and all.

If you are anything like me you have had the experience, hopefully not too many times, of letting down your hair, dropping your guard, taking off the mask, revealing the real you and living to regret it. Perhaps you assumed you shared something in confidence only to hear it around the church. Take courage, it happens to the best of us. But it is no reason to live a life of self-imposed exile or hide behind a mask.

God never meant for His children to rely solely upon Him to the exclusion of others. Six times within the creation story God sees what He has made and declares it, "Good!" The first time something is not good is that man was alone. *"It is not good for the man to be alone"* (Genesis 2:18a). It is through others that God meets our need for fellowship, intimacy, accountability, and help.

At the urging of my friend I went to that designer clothing outlet to add to my wardrobe. Baring myself was part of the process. God who is the Master Designer, has a custom-fitted wardrobe for every believer. Stripped of our own coverings, He clothes us in robes of righteousness and crowns our head with glory and honor. As we trust God to supply our every need, we will find that He can be trusted to send safe people into our lives before whom we can be naked and unashamed.

Prayer

Dear Lord, I pray healing for the pastor's wife who has been wounded. Bind up the breaks in her heart and wipe the tears from her eyes. To the one who grieves in Zion, I pray Your comforting presence and a safe person with whom she can be real. Amen

12

Naked and Unashamed

"One day we'll look back on this and laugh." A girlfriend and I tried in vain to comfort each other with these words. Somehow our much-anticipated dream get-away left us feeling trapped in a never-ending nightmare.

We chose to celebrate our friendship with a weekend of pampering in California's bucolic Napa Valley. The Napa region is lush and beautiful, known for its many vineyards and wineries. It is also known for its mineralized springs and mud baths. People also visit the area to see Old Faithful—a natural hot water geyser that erupts about every 30 minutes. Napa seemed the obvious locale for rest, relaxation, and rejuvenation.

We happily checked into a resort boasting over 50 years of experience in providing natural, simple relaxation. Once it had even been featured on the old television show

Lifestyles of the Rich and Famous. Feeling like celebrities, we signed up for "The Works." Spa attendants who spoke in pleasant hushed voices filled our arms with oversized, fluffy towels, while instructing us on where to disrobe and stow our belongings. We masked our shock at the openness of the changing room behind timid smiles and, along with several other women, hurried out of our clothes and into the safety and privacy of the oversized towels. I wondered if the resort's rich and famous clients had to undress before strangers.

Swaddled in our terrycloth cocoons and sipping mineral water, we sat outside the large tiled treatment room while waiting for our personal attendants. Once when the door opened I caught sight of a heavyset naked woman mincing by. Behind my cup of water I whispered to my friend, "She sure is free." Giggling like girls, it never occurred to me that in a matter of moments I would be the naked lady on the other side of the door.

Once inside the first words I heard were, "I'll take your towel." Thus the nightmare began. For the next few hours I endured varying forms of shame, humiliation, and exposure. Under the watchful eye of my fully clothed attendant, I was told to step into the shower, which turned out to be a showerhead mounted on the wall. Without benefit of a stall, curtain, or partition of any kind, who cares that the water is mineralized? Then it was on to the mud bath. At least I had something to get in and cover myself with.

After the mud bath it was back to the cleansing mineral water shower followed by the "bubbling aromatic mineral bath." Although I was in a tub within a stall—there was no door! With so many women walking back and forth I felt like a nude mannequin in a department store window on Fifth Avenue.

The natural mineral steam room—let's just say it was like being in a hot, steamy hut on the set of a National Geographic photo shoot. While inside, a small window opened and my attendant handed me a dampened, rolled hand towel filled with ice chips. The other women used their towels to cool their brows. I promptly shook my ice onto the floor of the hut and covered myself as best I could with the towel, ignoring the stares of my "bosom buddies."

The Works ended with a blanket wrap, cool down, and massage. Finally, covers!

I never thought I'd experience anything like that again. But I have, many times, when I joined an accountability and prayer group. These women were warm, welcoming, and obviously used to parading around naked before each other. Although fully clothed, within this safe, loving, godly environment these women unashamedly shed masks as well as tears. They readily revealed those thing we tend to hide—fears, insecurities, weaknesses, and besetting sins.

Week after week, for months and then years, I faithfully attended. Initially I was shocked and often thought about the heavyset naked woman at the spa. These women were also free. The things they expressed and exposed before one another was more than I cared to see or hear about. For weeks on end I thought there's no way I could ever be so forthcoming. But they led by example and pretty soon I felt self-conscious being so "overdressed." Little by little I learned to "disrobe," get beneath the surface stuff and get real. Scripture tells us that is how we receive healing.

"Is any one of you in trouble? [S]he should pray. Is anyone happy? Let [her] sing songs of praise. Is any one of you sick? [S]he should call the elders of the church to pray over [her] and anoint [her] with oil in the name of the Lord. And the prayer offered in faith will make the sick person well; the Lord will raise [her] up. If [s]he has sinned, [s]he will be forgiven. Therefore confess your sins to each other and pray for each other so that you may be healed. The prayer of a righteous [wo]man is powerful and effective" (James 5:13-16 NIV).

Pastors' wives, of all people, need a safe place where we can de-stress, relax, and rejuvenate. Despite the fact that others put us on pedestals, we know that we are not perfect, nor do we have it all together. But where can we go? Who can be trusted to bear our burdens? Who will still love us once they've seen us naked?

I'm here to remind you of another Old Faithful. *"Jesus Christ is the same yesterday and today and forever"* (Hebrews 13:8 NIV). He offers living water that cleanses from sin, washes whiter than snow, and restores weary souls.

If you're willing to step outside of your comfort zone and trust Him, the Lord will lead you to those with whom you can be naked and unashamed. For others, perhaps these words are God's way of reminding you that He wants you to start just such a group. If so, I have two words for you. Trust! Obey!

Initially there will be the awkwardness and uneasiness at disrobing before others. Baring one's true self to another takes time. But if you trust and obey, you will experience a deeper more intimate level of loving fellowship with God and others. Your healing will appear and you will be like a well-watered garden, like a spring whose waters never fail. (Isaiah 58:8, 11).

13

Conquering Comparison

T he woman I listened to on the phone tearfully related how inferior she felt to the other students in her Bible class, largely made up of fellow church members– young and old, professionals and plain old Joes, Ph.D.'s and "GED's."

When the instructor asked questions or called for comments, if a "professional" responded, this precious sister clammed up, retreating to the inner recesses of her thickening shell. Week after week this was her practice. An unwilling captive of comparison, imprisoned by tormenting thoughts of inadequacy and failure, she wavered between finishing the course and quitting.

A teen girl, straight-A student, recipient of numerous awards and scholarships, who has the looks and poise of a model, struggles with feeling bad about herself and is often unaware of her abilities. While digging to find the root of her discontent she surprised me with a ready response, "I know why I feel this way... I'm comparing myself to others."

Sadly, I've had similar conversations with many women, including ministry wives. One bright, articulate ministry wife felt "less than" because she is not college educated.

Being in the company of ministry wives who have college and/or seminary degrees caused her to regret having made a different educational and career choice many years ago. When consumed with comparing herself to others, she lost sight of her giftedness and God-given ability to minister effectively. However, when this ministry wife confronted comparison as sin and repented of how she let it control her life, a newfound freedom and self-acceptance was discovered.

When we struggle with comparison, we are usually comparing our weaknesses to the strengths of another. Consequently we mistakenly assume others think or feel about us the way we think or feel about ourselves.

God told Moses to send men to explore the land of Canaan, which He promised to give to the Israelites. Moses chose 12 leaders to explore Canaan and come back with a thorough report of the land, its produce, the people and their villages. Although the men came back boasting of the land's bounty, they were fearful of its inhabitants. *"The land we explored devours those living in it. All the people we saw there are of great size...We seemed like grasshoppers in our own eyes, and we looked the same to them"* (Numbers 13:32, 33b).

By comparing themselves to the inhabitants of Canaan, the Israelites lost sight of who they were, whose they were, and God's promise to give them the land. Their fear led to faithlessness and disbelief, which caused God to become angry with them. *"How long will this people treat me with contempt? How long will they refuse to believe in Me, in spite of all the miraculous signs I have performed among them"* (Numbers 14:11)?

By comparing ourselves to other women we, too, can lose sight of who we are, whose we are, and the promises and plans God gives us. Fear of not measuring up can lead to faithlessness and disbelief, born of discouragement. It also grieves the Holy Spirit.

Before you can ever find and enjoy fulfillment as a Christian woman, you must know who you are. There will always be the inner and outer voices telling you who you should be and what you should be doing. Resisting the temptation to listen to and heed those voices will keep you from the frustration of spinning off into a thousand different destructive directions.

Whenever someone shares with me their struggle with comparison, I share with them the following Scriptures: *"We do not dare to classify or compare ourselves with some who commend themselves. When they measure themselves by themselves and compare themselves with themselves, they are not wise. But, 'Let him who boasts, boast in the Lord.' For it is not the one who commends himself who is approved, but the one whom the Lord commends"* (2 Corinthians 10:12, 17-18). "[Sisters] *think of what you were when you were called. Not many of you were wise by human standards; not many were influential; not many were of noble birth. But God chose the foolish things of the world to shame the wise; God chose the weak things of the world to shame the strong. He chose the lowly things of this world and the despised things – and the things that are not – to nullify the things that are, so that no one may boast before Him. It is because of Him that you are in Christ Jesus, who has become for us wisdom from God – that is our righteousness, holiness and redemption. Therefore, as it is written: 'Let him who boasts boast in the Lord'"* (1 Corinthians 1:26-31).

Remember the 12 explorers Moses chose to spy out Canaan? Two of the 12, Joshua and Caleb, brought back a different report. Believing God's promise to give them the land, Caleb said, *"We should go up and take possession of the land, for we can certainly do it... The land we passed through and explored is exceedingly good. If the Lord is pleased with us, He will lead us into that land, a land flowing with milk and honey, and will give it to us. Only do not rebel against the LORD. And do not be afraid of the people of the land, because we will swallow them up. Their protection is gone, but the LORD is with us. Do not be afraid of them"* (Numbers 13:30; 14:7-9).

I challenge you to become like Joshua and Caleb who, despite their circumstances, believed God. If you believe God's Word and act upon it, you too can conquer comparison.

14

Dealing With Betrayal

John 13

At a recent communion service, I listened intently to the words my husband spoke. "On the night that He was betrayed, our Lord, with His disciples gathered around Him in an upper room in Jerusalem, took bread, broke it and gave to His disciples saying, This is My body which is broken for you. Eat this in remembrance of Me..."

Those familiar words, taken from the account we commonly refer to as The Last Supper, suddenly took on deeper meaning. The opening words arrested me—On the night that He was betrayed... On the night that He was *betrayed*... Betrayed!

Knowing what would shortly and inevitably take place as the direct result of His betrayal, our Savior followed the plan through to the end and purchased our salvation with His life. With renewed awe, reverence and gratitude,

I received the bread and the cup...those words continuing to sound in my head, '*On the night that He was betrayed...*'

Now I don't know about you but if I had foreknowledge of my betrayal by one of my guests—supper would be off! Sadly I'd want to say, "Brothers, remember the last time we ate together? *That* was the last supper. John, stop leaning on me. Right now I've got the weight of the world on my shoulders and I don't need you, too. As a matter of fact, everyone, please leave!" And that's just putting it mildly.

The word betray defined by Webster's New World Dictionary means:

1   *a*) to help the enemy of (one's country, cause, etc.); be a traitor to *b*) to deliver or expose to an enemy traitorously

2   to break faith with; fail to meet the hopes of; he *betrayed* my trust in him"

3   to lead astray; deceive; specifically, to seduce and then desert[8]

Christian counselor, author and speaker Dr. Dan Allender says, "Betrayal is any disregard or harm done to the dignity of another... Betrayal, thus defined, is a constant wound inflicted in all relationships. It is such a normal part of life that our attention is hardly drawn to the casual, innocuous betrayals of everyday interactions, that is, unless serious betrayal has occurred that predisposes a person toward vigilant scrutiny and jaundiced perception...The damage of betrayal is the deepening conviction that relationships can neither be enjoyed, trusted, nor expected to last."[9]

Being a Christian does not exempt us from experiencing the pain of betrayal, neither does being a pastor's wife—nor did being the Son of God. Yet, if we look carefully at the life of Jesus and the events leading up to and just following His betrayal, we too can learn how to battle betrayal and live an overcoming life.

Of all the Gospels, the 13th chapter of John gives the longest and most insightful account of the events that occurred in the upper room on the night of Jesus' betrayal. It also records many insights into Jesus' character. He is our Perfect Example in all things. By examining His life let's see how we measure up.

> *"... Until we all reach unity in the faith and in the knowledge of the Son of God and become mature, attaining to the whole measure of the fullness of Christ"* (Ephesians 4:13).

On the night that He was betrayed:

> *"...Having loved his own who were in the world, he [Jesus] now showed them the full extent of his love"* (John 13:1b).

To what extent do you show love to others, especially those who've betrayed you?

"...He got up from the meal, took off his outer clothing, and wrapped a towel around his waist. After that, he poured water into a basin and began to wash his disciples' feet, drying them with the towel that was wrapped around him...When he finished washing their feet, he put on his clothes and returned to his place...Now that I, your Lord and Teacher, have washed your feet, you also should wash one another's feet. I have set you an example that you should do as I have done for you...Now that you know these things, you will be blessed if you do them"
(John 13:4-5, 12, 14, 17).

The washing of feet was a menial task typically performed by a servant. In washing the feet of His disciples Jesus modeled humility and the heart of a servant. How do you feel or respond when *treated* as a servant?

In verses 18-30 Jesus expresses knowledge of His betrayal, yet, He does not expose the one who would betray Him. Instead he gives Judas opportunity to repent, even breaking bread with him—which was a sign of close fellowship. Jesus did not regard Judas as an enemy. Prior to hand-picking his disciples, Jesus spent a night in prayer. Judas was handpicked. Although appearing trustworthy, Judas was dishonest (John 12:4-6). Sometimes saints behave as "ain'ts". How do you regard those who've betrayed you? Do you expose them and their deeds to others? Or, like Jesus, do you provide them with space to repent?

Battling betrayal is neither easy nor painless. It cost Jesus his life. However, by overcoming death He also overcame betrayal...and so can we. As Jesus told His disciples, *"A new command I give you: Love one another. As I have loved you, so you must love one another. By this all men will know that you are My disciples, if you love one another"* (John 13:34-35).

15

Healing From Betrayal

M uch like physical wounds, emotional wounds can fester, grow, and cause great damage if not treated properly. Healing, however, is possible, though not always pain-free.

The Greek word for betray, paradidomi, comes from the two words para and didomi. Para is a prefix most often attached to verbs and means near, beside, side by side, in the vicinity of, at, in proximity to. Didomi is a verb meaning to give or bring forth, commit, deliver (up or to an enemy), have power, smite (with the hand), strike (with the palm of the hand), suffer, yield. The combination of the two words suggests nearness or closeness of one who, through such proximity, has the power to harm another in a number of ways.

The actual or assumed closeness we feel toward another is what makes betrayal so hurtful. We are not surprised

63

when an enemy or stranger betrays us. However, betrayal from someone close—a friend, neighbor, confidant, family member, etc., has the power to wound deeply. King David experienced such betrayal and said, *"Even my close friend, whom I trusted, he who shared my bread, has lifted up his heel against me"* (Psalm 41:9).

Here are several practical points for help in overcoming betrayal:

- **Take your pain to God.**

Sometimes we think it best to act super spiritual and that we're above being hurt. When Jesus was betrayed, Scripture says, *"They went to a place called Gethsemane, and Jesus said to his disciples," Sit here while I pray..." He began to be deeply distressed and troubled and said, "My soul is overwhelmed with sorrow to the point of death..." Going a little farther, he fell to the ground and prayed..."* (Mark 14:32-35).

"For we have not a high priest who is unable to sympathize with our weaknesses, but we have one who has been tempted in every way, just as we are—yet without sin. Therefore, let us approach the throne of grace with confidence, so that we may receive mercy and find grace to help us in our time of grief" (Hebrews 4:15-16).

- **Settle your differences according to Scripture.**

After taking your pain to God, He commands you to go to the one who has betrayed you. Direct any anger towards the issue, not the person.

"In your anger do not sin. Do not let the sun go down while you are still angry, and do not give the devil a foothold" (Ephesians 4:26-27).

If the offending party doesn't receive you or reconciliation is not achieved, take an objective, spiritually mature person with you. If the offender is still not open to reconciliation, love them from afar. *"If your brother sins against you, go and show him his fault, just between the two of you. If he listens to you, you have won your brother over. But if he will not listen, take one or two others along, so that every matter may be established by the testimony of two or three witnesses. If he refuses to listen to them, tell it to the church; and if he refuses to listen even to the church, treat him as you would a pagan or a tax collector... Then Peter came to Jesus and asked, "Lord, how many times shall I forgive my brother when he sins against me? Up to seven times?" Jesus answered, "I tell you not seven times, but seventy-seven times"* (Matthew 18: 15-22).

- **Be careful concerning what you say or don't say about the offender.**

Be a good steward over your words. Refuse to practice slander or participate in gossip. *"Do not let any unwholesome talk come out of your mouths, but only what is helpful for building others up according to their needs, that it may benefit those who listen... Get rid of all bitterness, rage and anger, brawling and slander, along with every form of malice"* (Ephesians 4:29-31).

- **Allow love to cover what you could expose.**

Christian counselor, author and speaker Dr. Dan Allender says, "To love is to be more committed to the other than we are to the relationship, to be more concerned about his or her walk with God than the comfort or benefits of his or her walk with us." This is easier said than done, but like most other things, practice makes perfect. *"Above all, love each other deeply, because love covers over a multitude of sins"* (1 Peter 4:8).

- **Remember, God is the Great Physician and Healer.**

He longs to bind up every painful break in your heart and relationships, to liberate and free you from the captivity of unforgiveness and negative emotions and release you from the dark prison of bitterness and depression, to comfort you when you mourn and provide for you as you grieve—to bestow on you a crown of beauty instead of ashes, the oil of gladness instead of mourning, and a garment of praise instead of a spirit of despair. (See Isaiah 61:1-3)

16

Army Wives

While clicking the television's remote control and scrolling through show after show, I happened upon a movie called Army Wives. Being the precursor to a new series, the movie ended with several unfinished stories centering upon the lives of four army spouses and life on an army base.

Army Wives featured an incredible amount of preposterous drama jam-packed into 90 minutes. Fortunately, even with unfinished storylines to ensure weekly viewers, bonds formed among the spouses living on base. No matter what the situation—new marriage, surrogate pregnancy, adoption, domestic violence, post-traumatic stress disorder, deployment, or death—there was always a seasoned spouse close by offering support and encouragement.

I was hooked, not by the storyline but by the, albeit Hollywood-style, friendships formed within 90 minutes.

By the end of the movie those budding bonds were in full bloom. I envied their ease of development. Yes, there were challenges galore, after all this was a made-for-TV movie, but each one was overcome or made bearable by those willing to help shoulder the load. It left me wondering about my life and relationships, and those of other pastors' wives.

The army has a volunteer organization called Army Family Team Building (AFTB) whose objective is "to provide training, knowledge, and skills to prepare soldiers' spouses and family members for all aspects and stages of Army life. The program's focus is to empower and encourage family members to be self-sufficient and mission-ready." AFTB understands that "strong families are the pillars of support behind strong soldiers."

Volunteerism is an outstanding aspect of AFTB. Their website even says, "Getting involved in your Army community has an enormous impact on one's experience with Army life. By getting to know others in your community you'll feel empowered in your military lifestyle and be better prepared for anything that might come your way."

AFTB addresses such areas as: Army basics, expectations and impact on family life, child and youth services, home and family life, moving/relocating, managing deployment, money matters, senior spouse support services, benefits and entitlements, etc.

I can almost hear some of you say, "I wish I had something like that. Pastors' families need an AFTB, after all we are soldiers in the army of the Lord!" And that's so true. Just as the government's call upon a soldier impacts his or her family, so God's call upon a minister impacts his or her family. Therefore, connecting with others of like precious faith is vital to one's own survival.

I've said it before and I'll say it again and again, "It takes one to know one. We are our best resource." Scripture says, *"The way God designed our bodies is a model for understanding our lives together as a church: every part dependent on every other part, the parts we mention and the parts we don't, the parts we see and the parts we don't see. If one part hurts, every other part is involved in the hurt, and in the healing. If one part flourishes, every other part enters into the exuberance"* (1 Corinthians 12: 25-26 MSG).

Knowing the oft-expressed loneliness and isolation of being a pastors' wife, you have probably asked yourself, "To whom can I reach out?" or "Who can I bless?" It may begin as simply as praying for another pastor's wife.

My husband answered the call to pastor a church in California, 3,000 miles away from our childhood homes in Pennsylvania. I longed desperately for connection, to know and be known by others. I loved the Lord but not my lonely lot in life. No other woman in our congregation was in my shoes and therefore, I reasoned, they were unable to relate to certain levels of my loneliness. So, I decided to throw a party—a pity party. Only one guest showed up and He wasn't even invited. God knows our need for connection, fellowship, love, and support. Why not trust Him with your life while seeking to bless someone else's?

Praying for pastors' wives gave birth to a ministry, Wives In Touch, and resulted in rich relationships with other "army" wives. Look to the Lord and ask Him how to reach out to another pastor's wife or a trustworthy sister. You will be amazed at how He meets your needs as you seek to meet the needs of another. I am living proof!

17

Reach Out and Touch Someone

~~~~~

Have you ever taken notice of how many different conferences are available for so many different groups and interests of people? The numbers are staggering. Thankfully, even pastors' wives are gathering together more often. However, I remember when that was not the case. This sacred sorority used to seem like a secret sorority.

In the book *Help! I'm a Pastor's Wife*, contributing author Jean Coleman writes: *Pastors' wives are often victims of the Elijah syndrome. They feel so isolated and alone that eventually they cry out, "I, even I only, am left!" There seems to be no one who understands, no one who can appreciate her unique problems. It is tempting to sit down under a juniper tree and give up!*[10]

One year I received an invitation to attend a service just for pastors' wives. It was one of the special events planned during an international church conference. I could hardly wait to go. My imagination swirled with anticipation as I envisioned meeting my sisters and engaging in rich, deep fellowship.

After experiencing several airport delays, storms, and flights, the day of the service finally arrived. I took my place among several hundred pastors' wives from around the world. We flowed into the sanctuary and filled the pews. The worship leader led us in song and into the presence of the Father. Our blended voices filled the air with melodic praise.

The guest speaker stirred our pure minds by reminding us of how very special we are to God. We were encouraged to remain faithful to Him because He is faithful, able, and anxiously awaiting to perform the impossible in our lives, as we walk in obedience and become women of prayer. Again and again we were challenged to be God's servants; those who seek His face and search His heart. Because our hearts will be forever restless until we find our rest in Him.

What an awesome word! And yet, in the midst of that wonderful service, we sat together, alone. We sang with each other but failed to speak to each other. I kept wondering if eye contact was avoided to keep from seeing or revealing that which pastors' wives become so adept at hiding.

An altar call was made but no one moved, although some sat weeping in solitary silence. After the benediction we gathered our belonging into our arms, barely exchanging glances, and hurried away. How much better it would have been if we had gathered one another into our arms and exchanged names and contact information. I left sad and disappointed. Pastors' wives cry out for times of refreshing with other sisters of like precious faith and calling, and then fail to make the most of a God-sent opportunity. Why? What do we fear?

Jean Coleman experienced a similar situation while preparing to host a gathering for pastors' wives. She writes, *"I spent my time on my knees seeking the Lord for a format for the gathering. It seemed that what we needed more than anything else was simply an opportunity to communicate with one another... What I really wanted was for the Holy Spirit to be in charge... I was to be the hostess; He was to act as moderator. I wanted everyone to feel free to say what was on her heart.*

My part was easy—the battle took place with the individual wives. There were many fears to overcome. Pastors' wives can be very timid women. So many are used to staying in the background and not really taking much initiative. [Traveling] alone...into new territory presented a real challenge to many wives. Walking into a room where they would probably know no one at all was another stumbling block.

Even mixing with charismatics and those from denominations other than their own was a mighty mountain to move.

It was easier to make an excuse and relax in the security of the dark cave than to walk across the water. But God was in it, and the Holy Spirit was drawing us together. He has a way of making confetti out of our excuses when He wants to build His body together in unity."

God knows our desire and need for fellowship with other pastors' wives. He is raising up women to facilitate just such gatherings. After many tears, much prayer, planning, and preparation, conferences for pastors' wives are truly beginning to emerge. I received a letter from a precious sister in Lake Charles, LA. She wrote, *"...I recently attended a women's conference featuring a session for pastors' wives. I must say that I was truly blessed. This was the first time I had attended a conference that had a special session for pastors' wives. What a wonderful way to teach us and reach us and just to bring us together..."*

I believe that through these types of conferences, gatherings, and networking sessions, our God will do immeasurably more than all we ask or imagine, according to His power that is at work within us.

And if by chance I'm blessed with the good fortune of meeting you, I promise to look you in the eye, gather you in my arms, exchange names and contact information, because I'd love to keep in touch!

Up Close
and Personal

18

Managing Those Martha Moments

L iving in California and learning of the severe drought conditions, I was prompted to do my part in conserving water. Instead of using the dishwasher I washed dishes by hand. When doing laundry I saved the water from the final rinse cycles. This was used to water the shrubs and trees surrounding our home and for washing the cars. After several years of doing this I tired of the added work. On laundry days I became grumpy and complained of all the work I did all by myself. I was worse in the evenings after washing the dinner dishes.

In my frustration I thought, God, nobody even cares that I do all this work. Paul could help if he wasn't so *busy* playing with the kids. I don't want to nag him so please move on his heart to help me.

The work I did was self-imposed so no one felt sorry for me. When the family offered to help, if they didn't save the water, I refused their services. Initially the motivation behind my actions was water conservation. But somewhere along the way I lost sight of the motive and became overwhelmed with the task.

Feeling frustrated and defeated I began using the dishwasher. The time and effort it saved me left me relaxed and eager to do things with the family that previously I had been too tired to do. I was playful, pleasant, and happy... and everybody noticed.

Being married to the pastor makes me well aware of his concerns. When there are jobs to be done I often volunteer to help out. But just like saving the water, work becomes a burden when working for the wrong reason or with the wrong attitude. Luke 10:38-42 accurately describes this dilemma.

Martha desired to minister to Jesus and his disciples. She voluntarily invites them to her home but soon becomes overwhelmed with the necessary preparations. In her frustration Martha cries out to the Lord but for the wrong reason. First, she accuses Him of not caring for her, "*...Lord, don't you care...*" Then she accuses her sister of not being as busy as she, "*...My sister has left me to do the work by myself...*" Lastly, Martha begins ordering Jesus, "*...Tell her to help me!*"

Distracted by her much service for the Lord, Martha is drawn away from Him instead of being drawn to Him.

Working for the Lord while being preoccupied with what needs to be done (and with those who aren't doing it) only leads to frustration and feeling overwhelmed in doing good works. Just as Jesus spoke to Martha He's had to say to me, "Meredith, Meredith, you are worried and upset about many things, but only one thing is needed...rest.

As pastors' wives, whether we volunteer, get drafted, or are led of the Lord to serve within the congregation, Jesus, not the task, must always be our focus. Spending time in His presence allows us to rest from our busyness. In Scripture we often find Jesus stealing away from the people and their needs in order to spend time resting and being refreshed by God. Jesus teaches His disciples to do likewise, *"Then, because so many people were coming and going that they did not even have a chance to eat, he said to them, "Come with me by yourselves to a quiet place and get some rest""* (Mark 6:31 NIV).

When we spend time in God's presence we are restored and refreshed to be of even greater service to Him. Mary modeled this before her sister Martha. May you be encouraged to rest at the feet of the Master.

19

Relationships

Relationships are God's idea. Since the creation of Adam, man has had the privilege of a relationship with God. With the creation of woman God set the stage for the birthing of every other type of relationship: marriage, family, community, friendship, etc.

My husband often teaches on relationships and says there are three types every maturing believer should have: 1) those *to whom* we minister, 2) those *with whom* we minister, and 3) those who minister to us. It is God's will that our lives reflect a healthy balance of all three.

Pastors' wives are often sought out for a variety of relationships. Therefore it is necessary that we be prayerful, open, and discerning in order to know how best to go about establishing and maintaining them. In her book *The Friendships of Women*, Dee Brestin writes, *"Being alert to the possibility that God may bring a person across our path will change our attitude toward first meetings. We may capture beautiful friendships that in time past would have slipped away."[11]*

As I take inventory of my relationships I am grateful to God for the many wonderful people who are a part of my life. First, there are those to whom I minister. Many of them are younger women who need a shoulder to cry on, a listening ear, words of encouragement, or loving counsel. Titus 2:3-5 says, *"Teach the older women to be reverent in the way they live...to teach what is good. Then they can train the younger women..."*

Then there are those with whom I minister. A definite part of maturity is learning to cooperate as well as operate. I've served as the primary leader of our church's women's fellowship, but this branch of ministry would suffer greatly were it not for faithful women who work alongside me. Solomon declared, *"Two are better than one, because they have a good return for their work: If one falls down, his friend can help him up! Also, if two lie down together, they will keep warm. But how can one keep warm alone? Though one may be overpowered, two can defend themselves. A cord of three strands is not quickly broken"* (Ecclesiasts 4:9-12).

Finally, there are those who minister to me. Proverbs 27:17 says, "As iron sharpens iron, so one man sharpens another." There are those who admonish, challenge, encourage, nourish, and support me. In developing these intimate relationships I have had to take risks to become vulnerable and transparent before another.

When my family and I moved to California I lacked intimate relationships with other women, especially pastors' wives. Wives In Touch was conceived during that time. It was then that I learned to be faithful in ministering to and with others and to trust God to meet my own need. I also learned a lot about myself, things that could either enhance or hinder the kind of relationship I sought.

In the book *Can I Afford Time For Friendships?*, former pastor's wife and author Colleen Evans says, *"If you're currently without a close intimate friend then examine yourself. Is it a case of timing, or is the reason behind this lack in your life of your own doing? With open and honest communication between you and the Lord, ask for insights into what you need to change to make space for someone special within your heart. Then give yourself time to change certain traits that need changing."*[12] God knows the unique needs of pastors' wives and has promised to supply them all.

"And my God will meet all your needs according to his glorious riches in Christ Jesus" (Philippians 4:19).

20

Living a Balanced Life

P astors' wives are often sought out for counsel, words of encouragement, or prayer. These can be wonderful opportunities of rich spiritual development both in the individual with needs and also in us. However, if we are not adequately maintaining a balance between our personal and ministry life, we can easily feel we have nothing left to give.

First Kings 17:7-16 tells the story of a widow woman who is commanded by God to feed the prophet Elijah. When Elijah asks her for water and then bread she responds by saying, *"As surely as the Lord your God lives, I don't have any bread—only a handful of flour in a jar and a little oil in a jug. I am gathering a few sticks to take home and make a meal for myself and my son, that we may eat it—and die."*

Elijah's request is not outrageous. He asks the woman to make him a small cake of bread. However, this woman is facing starvation. For her a small cake of bread represents everything she has.

Some time ago I felt spiritually drained. I thought about that widow. When asked to pray or counsel with someone, inwardly I cried, "As surely as the Lord God lives, I don't have any counsel—only my notes from Sunday's message written on the back of the bulletin, that I've somehow misplaced. I am looking for them to make a devotional for myself, that I may feed upon it lest I die."

Eventually I went to the Great Physician with symptoms including exhaustion, weakness, loss of appetite, sudden bursts of tears, and caring for others but not caring for myself. After a prayerful examination it was determined that my run-down condition was due to an imbalanced spiritual diet—too much fast food, eating on the run or skipping meals, too little living water, and insufficient rest in the Lord.

Immediately I began following my "doctor's orders" and adhered to a strict diet. By feeding daily on God's word I began to fill out, develop, and put on weight spiritually. Resting in God's presence restores and refreshes. Time spent with Him allows for the stillness needed to properly order my day. God fills the weary soul with His peace in the midst of all that clamors for our attention.

In the church where I grew up we sang a song entitled Take Time To Be Holy. One verse begins with, *"Take time to be holy, the world rushes on..."* Sometimes we get caught in a similar rushed lifestyle. We hurry here and there doing so many good things but nothing can take the place of spending quality and quantity time with the Lord.

Jesus confronted Martha about her busyness but commended her sister Mary saying, *"She has chosen what is better, and it will not be taken away from her."* What was Mary doing? Sitting at the feet of Jesus—listening (Luke 10:42).

When the demands of ministry became too much for the disciples, Jesus told them to come away and rest. *"Then, because so many people were coming and going that they did not even have a chance to eat, He said to them, "Come with me by yourselves to a quiet place and get some rest"* (Mark 6:31).

Come away with God, regularly, and rest. Like the widow woman, we will find that once rested, God gives us the resources to feed others, our family, and ourselves. *"For the jar of flour was not used up and the jug of oil did not run dry, in keeping with the word of the Lord..."* (1 Kings 17:16).

21

Stand By Your Man

W henever there is an upcoming presidential election, much prying and spying goes on into the lives of the candidates. Years ago I read a published article regarding Bill Clinton's chances for re-election. One sentence in particular stood out. *"The head of the Whitewater hearings...has zeroed in on Hillary Clinton as the surest way to damage the President."* As a pastor's wife, statements like that grab my attention.

While pondering the sentiment expressed in that article, I thought, suppose Satan zeroes in on pastors' wives as the surest way to damage the pastor. I believe he often does.

Since the beginning of time Satan has gone through women to get to men. Let's look at a few examples. In the book of Genesis we see the first woman God created being charmed and deceived by Satan. Eve listened to Satan and began to doubt God's word. By listening to his wife, Adam introduced sin and death into the world.

Judges 13-16 tells the story of Samson. Samson was conceived under divine circumstances—his mother was barren (Judges 13:3). He was consecrated to God's service from birth and endowed with supernatural strength. God was the source of Samson's strength, but Samson was weak when it came to women. By consorting with the wrong women Samson was unaware that he was betraying his calling. When God's anointing left Samson he became a prisoner of the enemy.

King Solomon was said to have been greater in riches and wisdom than all the other kings of the earth. However, he too had a weakness for women. God told him not to intermarry with "foreign" women because they would surely turn his heart after other gods. First Kings 11:2-4 records Solomon's response to God's command. *"Nevertheless, Solomon held fast to them in love...and his wives led him astray. As Solomon grew old, his wives turned his heart after other gods, and his heart was not fully devoted to the Lord his God..."*

In these three instances we can clearly see how Satan baited his traps with women to ensnare man. Unfortunately, I can remember far too many times when Satan was successful in using me to get to my husband. It is hardly a coincidence that arguments, like unpredicted storms, arise out of nowhere before Paul has to minister. When patience is running low and sensitivity is high, misunderstanding is sure to be the result.

Once my daughter asked, "Mommy, how come it seems like you're crabby and frustrated every Sunday morning?" And I don't know about you, but I run more pantyhose on Sundays than any other day of the week. Now I'm not trying to suggest that getting a run is in any way satanic, but sometimes that's all it takes to push me over the edge.

I had to begin searching out and shoring up the areas of my life through which Satan could gain easy access. First Peter 5:8-9 says, *"Be self-controlled and alert. Your enemy the devil prowls around like a roaring lion looking for someone to devour. Resist him, standing firm in the faith..."*

Another passage of Scripture talks about striking the shepherd to scatter the flock. This verse took on new meaning for me several years ago when I heard a self-proclaimed witch on a radio program. I listened in shock and horror as she calmly explained that the members of her coven pray and fast regularly against pastors' wives. They reason, and accurately so, that pastors' wives are the most direct link to their actual targets—pastors.

Such attempts to thwart God's work should not frighten but embolden us. As helpmeets and virtuous women we must stand against the enemy and walk in unity with our mates. As a result, God will be glorified and our pastor/

husbands will have full confidence in us, knowing we will do them good and not evil, all the days of our lives.

Remember, Satan will come against us but he must not be allowed to come between us.

22

Family Matters

I t is with repeated awe that I witness the expansion of a family and the accompanying display of love. Children are indeed a gift from God. Not only do the parents shower the new arrival with love and acceptance, but so do maturing siblings, extended family, and a host of friends.

With the birth of our first child, Paul and I experienced a love for and devotion to this little person that was unimaginable. Alicia was "perfect" in our eyes. Everything about her we loved and accepted, or at least patiently tolerated. It was no different with our second child, Aaron. Although distinctly different in temperament from his sister, Aaron was the recipient of the same intense love and devotion.

Watching our children grow and develop is still a delight. As parents we learned early on not to compare. In many ways our children are different as night and day. What remains the same, however, and beyond comparison, is our deepening love and enjoyment of these two amazing gifts from God.

Alicia and Aaron grew at different rates. One began cutting teeth at six months while the other had a big toothless grin at their first birthday. One talked in complete sentences before age two. The other, quiet and observant, talks when there is something worth saying. They exhibit differing tastes and interests, strengths and weaknesses. Still, they are part of one family, related by blood despite obvious differences.

Reflecting on our natural family has helped me immeasurably as I reflect on God's family—the Church, and specifically the congregations we've been blessed to serve. As a pastor's wife, I often feel like a spiritual mother to God's children. Unfortunately, I have not always been as loving, accepting, patient, or tolerant of them as I've been with my natural children. From time to time I find myself becoming critical, inwardly, of the following kinds of "kids."

Cry Babies and Fussy Babies: Those who are too easily upset and offended; given to temper tantrums. Being challenged to grow up in Christ and develop His character is, in their words and way of thinking, "too hard." Their favorite words are, "I can't."

The Problem Child: If it's not one thing it's another. This person suffers from a victim mentality. They keep a problem and rarely assume responsibility for their predicaments—it's always someone else's fault.

The Strong-Willed, Rebellious, Hard-Headed Child: In light of sound doctrine and loving discipline, this individual insists on pursuing the way that *seems* right to them, unknowing or uncaring that their way always ends in death.

Tattletales: Having an underdeveloped sense of agape love and loyalty, the talebearer causes much strife and family discord.

Picky Eaters: By the time they ought to be on solid food they still need milk. Some gag and choke on "gnats" but can swallow "camels."

This list could go on and on (just look over your church's membership directory). As my husband often says, "You can pick your friends but you're stuck with your relatives." We are one family, having many members. Even though some family members are more challenging than others, we are all in the family—and through the cross of Calvary, blood relatives.

Children are indeed a gift from God. His greatest gift to us is His Son, Jesus Christ. *"For God so loved the world that He gave His only begotten Son..."* (John 3:16a). It is this most precious Gift who enables us to love others in the family of God.

23

Feeding God's Flock

*"When Jesus landed and saw a large crowd, he had
compassion on them and healed their sick. As evening
approached, the disciples came to him and said, "This
is a remote place, and it's already getting late. Send
the crowds away, so they can go to the villages and
buy themselves some food." Jesus replied, "They do
not need to go away. You give them something to eat"*
(Matthew 14:14-16).

If you nursed any of your children, do you remember
the very first time? I'll never forget my thoughts and
feelings when the nurse handed me a hungry bundle and
said, "Mrs. Sheppard, it's time to feed your daughter." Panic,
self-consciousness, and fear flooded me. My mind began
to race. *I've never done this before. Reveal myself and feed
someone? I don't even have milk yet!*

Thankfully the nurse was very compassionate and understanding. Noting my apprehension, she brought me a video on breast-feeding. Leaving me with words of encouragement, the nurse pulled the curtain completely around my bed and left me to discreetly discover my amazing abilities.

By watching the video I gained a degree of confidence that enabled me to feed my grateful, hungry baby. Even though I didn't have milk, I had colostrum that was produced during pregnancy. Within a few days mature milk was produced along with the colostrum and by two weeks completely replaced it.

Nursing became natural. Frequent breast-feeding built a healthy milk supply. Milk was produced by supply and demand. The more often I nursed my baby the more milk there was. It is amazing to think that despite my timidity and lack of experience, I was well equipped for the job.

Although nursing days are now behind me, from time to time I still experience feelings of panic, self-consciousness, and fear. When changes occur within the congregation, I sometimes doubt my ability to effectively serve others. Because of the scrutiny that naturally comes with being the pastor's wife, fear and self-consciousness can sneak up on me when I least expect it. At those times I think...*I've never done this before. Reveal myself and serve others? What do I have to give?*

"Pastor's wife" is a role of honor and distinction—we minister to the minister. Unfortunately this role does not come with instructions or a job description. This can leave us wondering what to do and if we are doing it correctly.

When my husband assumed the role of senior pastor, I longed for the wisdom, fellowship, and encouragement of other pastors' wives. Much of this I found in books. Entire shelves of my home library are dedicated to books and magazines by, for, and about pastors' wives. I even have books about presidents' wives. These were all good for "jump-starting" my confidence. However, just like God equipped me to feed and care for my children, He equips us to feed and care for His children.

Of all the books I own, the one I read most is the Bible. It contains wonderful stories of ordinary people who, despite their inexperience, accomplished extraordinary works through God's enabling power.

When tempted to envy a pastor's wife who can sing well, play the piano, is a dynamic speaker, or prolific writer, I think of young David. Refusing King Saul's armor and sword, David successfully conquers Goliath armed with five stones and his own slingshot.

Sometimes Satan suggests my gifts and abilities are insufficient for the task at hand, whatever it may be. That's when I remember the young boy who offered his fish and loaves of bread to Christ, who used them to feed a multitude.

The 14th chapter of Mark tells the story of the woman with the alabaster box. This box contained expensive perfume that the woman used to anoint Jesus. Many who witnessed her act of loving service became indignant and rebuked her harshly. In response to their murmuring, Jesus said, *"Leave her alone, why are you bothering her? She has done a beautiful thing to me... **She has done what she could**...I tell you the truth, wherever the gospel is preached throughout the world, what she has done will also be told, in memory of her"* (Mark 14:1-9).

What a glorious testimony! To think we still hear and tell the story of that woman's service unto Christ. Had she become fearful or reluctant to serve due to the criticism of others, self-consciousness, or timidity, we would never know her story.

I once heard a fellow pastor's wife say, "The calling is the enabling." God knows what we are capable of doing, even though we may not know. But as we yield ourselves to Him, whatever the task, we can do all things through Christ who gives us the strength!

Prayer

Father, sometimes I feel insufficient and ill-equipped for the task at hand. Help me to look to You, my all-sufficient God, and rely upon Your strength. Amen

24

Offering Hospitality

T hrough the years I continue to learn about hospitality. My very first lesson, however, revealed just how inhospitable I was. Without a doubt I was a "Martha." Just like the woman in Luke 10:38-41, I'd open my home to others and immediately become distracted by all the necessary preparations. Then I'd become resentful of those who left me to do the work by myself. At the end of such days I always had a throbbing headache.

In desperation I turned to my prayer group and admitted how inept I was at offering hospitality without grumbling, as 1 Peter 4:9 exhorts. The second thing I learned about hospitality was praying for it is a lot like praying for patience, which seems to inevitably involve tribulation. As this faithful group of intercessors prayed for me, guests showed up at my door faster than I issued invitations.

I used to believe the words to the song, I'm Every Woman. Now I know, it's all a myth. Trying to keep my home looking like something from the pages of Better Homes and Gardens while trying to look like a top model and emulating Betty Crocker, June Cleaver, Martha Stewart, and Mother Teresa all rolled into one, makes me schizophrenic not "the hostess with the mostest."

Have you ever noticed that sometimes it takes being overwhelmed before you really start to learn? When overwhelmed with a task, I suddenly realize how limited and imperfect I am. Striving to accomplish well-intended deeds in my own strength guarantees losing sight of what should take priority.

Simply put, hospitality is sharing what you have with others. A beautiful home, gourmet meals, china, crystal, and linen are all lovely touches, but disposition is more important than decorative displays. Proverbs 17:1 says, *"Better a dry crust with peace and quiet than a houseful of feasting, with strife."*

Having fine things may be nice, but having Jesus is infinitely better. If I only share "things" with others without sharing Him, my hospitality is lacking. Sharing Jesus can be done in countless ways, all having to do with being rather than doing. Martha the Harried Hostess lost sight of that fact with her much doing. Her sister Mary sat at the feet of Jesus "being" and was commended for it.

When I find myself becoming distracted by all the necessary preparations of practicing hospitality I pray, "Lord, show me how to share You with my guests." It's amazing how that simple prayer redirects my focus. As I focus on Christ, my doing becomes an act of worship and I minister to Him as well as to my guests. *"So whether you eat or drink or whatever you do, do it all for the glory of God"* (1 Corinthians 10:31).

Hospitality often involves the guest sharing with the host. Jesus was an invited guest in the home of Mary and Martha. While Martha sought to serve Jesus, Mary sat and received from Him.

Following are some practical hospitality helps I've learned along the way:

- If you have a spare room or guest room, if possible, don't let it become the catch-all. When guests come, having to move all that "stuff" to other parts of the house is always a hassle. This room doesn't have to be fancy but functional, like the one prepared by the Shunamite woman for the prophet Elisha. *"Lets' make a small room...and put in it a bed and a table, a chair and a lamp"* (2 Kings 4:10).
- Have designated sets of bath towels and bed linens that are solely for company use. (Invest in machine washable mattress and pillow covers.)

- When time is of the essence I rely on foaming bathroom cleaners that also disinfect. For other rooms, I use all-purpose cleaners and dusting sprays. After one conscientious guest went through four rolls of toilet paper in a few days keeping the sink and tub clean, I started buying different size sponges, paper towels, and reusable all-purpose cloths (like Handi-Wipes) and keeping them in the bathroom cabinet.

- Start a Just In Case (JIC) Box of toiletries including new toothbrushes, shower caps, disposable razors, etc. Many items can be obtained in trial sizes. Picking up one or two each time you shop can quickly stock your box. Having a supply of first-aid items is also quite helpful. (Remember to keep an eye on expiration dates.)

- Collect some quick-fix recipes that can also make complete meals. For "emergencies" keep on hand: pastas, instant potatoes/rice, a wide variety of canned goods, baking mixes, and beverages. For those who'd rather spend time with their guests than in the kitchen, I recommend two cookbooks. 1) Cooking With Three Ingredients by Andrew Schloss and 2) The Back Of The Box Cookbook.

- Recommended Reading: Open Heart, Open Home by Karen Burton Mains and The Joy Of Hospitality by Dee Brestin

25

Home Sweet Home

Hospitality is a "big deal" to me because by temperament I am introverted and somewhat shy. Although I enjoy interaction with other people, it can be quite draining. To recover and recharge I *need* solitude and quiet. My husband is my opposite. Paul is an extrovert—naturally social and outgoing. He gets recharged by being with people. For years our differences made socializing and practicing hospitality challenging. If you find yourself similarly challenged, there is hope! Every born-again believer is, more or less, introverted or extroverted. However, as we walk in the Spirit we draw our energy from the same Source—Jesus Christ, not our temperament.

Several passages in the New Testament admonish Christians to practice hospitality. Webster's New Universal Unabridged Dictionary defines hospitality as: The friendly reception and treatment of guests or strangers, the quality or disposition of receiving and treating guests and strangers in a warm, friendly, generous way.

A simple, straightforward Scripture I especially like is Romans 12:13, *"Share with God's people who are in need. Practice hospitality."* The accompanying study note says, "The Christian has social responsibility to all people, but especially to other believers (see Galatians 6:10). And for you fellow introverts, 1 Peter 4:9, *"Offer hospitality to one another without grumbling."*

As we put the Word into practice we become more like Christ. The Holy Spirit transforms our temperament and empowers up to serve others. Just as miraculously, when we practice hospitality the Holy Spirit transforms our homes and thy become:

First Aid Stations: places where emergency aid or treatment is given to those who are hurting and in need of the Great Physician; where the broken-hearted receive healing, the blind receive sight, and those that are bruised find liberty. *"The Spirit of the Lord is upon me, because he hath anointed me to preach the gospel to the poor; he hath sent me to heal the brokenhearted, to preach deliverance to the captives, and recovering of sight to the blind, to set at liberty them that are bruised"* (Luke 4:18 KJV).

Havens: a place of calm and safety where weary, storm-tossed travelers can find rest. *"Come to me, all you* *who are weary and burdened, and I will give you rest*" (Matthew 11:28).

Lighthouses: towers or structures displaying the bright light of Jesus, guiding those on the sea of life away from danger. *"Ye are the light of the world. A city that is set on an hill cannot be hid. Neither do men light a candle, and put it under a bushel, but on a candlestick; and it giveth light unto all that are in the house. Let your light so shine before men, that they may see your good works and glorify your father which is in heaven"* (Matthew 5:14-16 KJV).

Shelters: a place where people who have been battered by the adverse circumstances of life can find protection, refuge, and aid. *"For I was hungry and you gave me something to eat, I was thirsty and you gave me something to drink, I was a stranger and you invited me in, I needed clothes and you clothed me, I was sick and you looked after me, I was in prison and you came to visit me"* (Matthew 25:35-36).

This brief list could go on and on. In short, when we open our hearts and homes in true hospitality, we welcome the Eminent Guest, Jesus Christ. He makes our homes a little like Heaven on Earth.

26

One is the Loneliest Number

A common complaint heard among pastors' wives is that of loneliness and isolation. To greater or lesser degrees, all of us have experienced a deep longing for someone with whom we can laugh, cry, talk intimately, and just share the real you. Some of us were warned away from establishing intimate relationships with women in our congregations. Others took a risk, reached out and experienced betrayal of confidences or simply unmet expectations. And still others may have a variety of relationships but most of them, although pleasant, are rather superficial. Therefore, to whom do we turn with our struggles, hurts, frustrations, etc.? I believe strongly, we turn to our loving Heavenly Father and to one another.

In the early eighties when I was new to marriage and ministry, I experienced tremendous challenges in both. Inexperience, hurt, fears, unresolved past issues, and simply not knowing what to do, where to go for help, or who to talk to, became an unbearable burden. One day in desperation I thought, *I'm going to pick up the phone, dial seven digits, and ask whoever answers if I may talk to them.* Not knowing what else to do, I did it!

Dragging the telephone cord across the room, I sat on the floor of my bedroom closet and closed the door. Hidden by the darkness, surrounded by shoes and dress hems—I dialed seven digits. (Granted, I know that was foolish and would NEVER do it again or advise anyone else to do likewise.)

When a pleasant-voiced woman answered, the dam of my emotions broke and came flooding out in a torrent of tears as I shared my struggles. She listened patiently and then asked if I knew her. Assuring her that I didn't and apologizing for calling, I recounted how I came to reach her. Again she asked, "Are you sure you don't know me?"

As only a loving Heavenly Father could orchestrate such events, I sat pouring out my heart and hurt to a sister in Christ and a fellow pastor's wife.

She shared wise counsel from the Word and then prayed with me. In an instant I became eternally convinced that pastors' wives need each other. We know intimately the highs and lows, trials and triumphs, well-tried roads and slippery slopes of ministry. In short, it takes one to know one.

Another time while attending a conference for pastors' wives, I reflected on pain from my past. Inwardly, I felt compelled to confess them. Because the thoughts were negative and painful, I assumed the feeling was either my flesh or the devil. Thankfully, the Lord reminded me that Christ was sent into the world to reveal, not conceal, that we may be healed. Again, I turned to a pastor's wife whose workshop I attended. God used her words to convey His loving counsel. Jean is a spiritually seasoned, maternal woman who happens to live 3,000 miles away. We met briefly at a conference but have corresponded for years. "*Confess to one another therefore your faults (your slips, your false steps, your offenses, your sins) and pray [also] for one another, that you may be healed and restored [to a spiritual tone of mind and heart]. The earnest (heartfelt, continued) prayer of a righteous man (or pastors' wife) makes tremendous power available [dynamic in its working]*" (James 5:16 AMP).

In Revelation 12:10 Satan is referred to as the accuser of the brothers who accuses them before our God day and night. Listen, he accuses sisters too! When we confess to one another the very thing Satan wants us to conceal, he no longer has the power to shame us. We begin to heal from the pain of our past when we speak out. Confess!

I met Linda through a mutual acquaintance. Linda is a Christian. Linda is a pastor's wife. She is also a registered nurse and a marriage and family therapist. Linda is my counselor. Once again, God has used a pastor's wife to walk with me and minister His healing...that I would be made whole and do likewise. My very first appointment with Linda was on a Tuesday. Between Tuesday and Saturday of that same week, four different women (three from my congregation and one a fellow pastor's wife) shared with me the same sort of things I shared with Linda.

Our Savior still cares for the multitudes and for the individual with what feels like a multitude of problems. The very things we try to discard or discount, Jesus says about them, *"Gather up now the fragments (the broken pieces that are left over), so that nothing may be lost or wasted"* (John 6:12 AMP). A songwriter echoed that sentiment when he wrote, "Heartaches, broken pieces, ruined lives are why You died on Calvary..."

The apostle Paul could have been writing expressly to pastors' wives: *Praise be to the God and Father of our Lord Jesus Christ, the Father of compassion and the God of all comfort, who comforts us in all our troubles, so that we can comfort those in any trouble with the comfort we ourselves have received from God. For just as the sufferings of Christ flow over into our lives, so also through Christ our comfort overflows. If we are distressed, it is for your comfort and salvation; if we are comforted, it is for your comfort, which produces in you patient endurance of the same sufferings we suffer. And our hope for you is firm, because we know that just as you share in our sufferings, so also you share in our comfort* (2 Corinthians 1:3-7 NIV).

A timeless tactic of the enemy is to divide and conquer. We do not have to grin and bear the oftentimes self-imposed loneliness and isolation plaguing pastors' wives. God never meant for us to bear our burdens alone.

> *"Two [pastors' wives] are better than one, because they have a good reward for their work: if one falls down [her] friend can help [her] up! Though one may be overpowered, two can defend themselves. A cord of three strands is not quickly broken"*
> (Ecclesiastes 4:9-10, 12 NIV).

Press on, beloved. I'm praying for you.

The
Journey Continues

27

Fighting the Good Fight of Faith

A long the road to fulfilling God's will one must continually overcome challenges, setbacks, discouragement, and opposition. Sometimes we err in thinking
opposition is God's way of telling us that what we're doing
must not be His will. Satan has a vested interest in our
believing that lie. He delights when we mistakenly forsake
a God-given task due to demonic opposition.

Webster's dictionary defines opposition as: 1) the action
of opposing (to stand in the way of; hinder; obstruct),
resisting, or combating. 2) antagonism or hostility. 3) a
person or group of people opposing, criticizing, or pro-
testing something or someone.

One summer God burdened me to pray for pastors'
wives experiencing opposition. Sometimes the opposition

we face is quite insidious—well hidden, yet advancing imperceptibly. Other times it's blatant—brazenly obvious and in your face. To overcome opposition it is important to remember, "*...our struggle is not against flesh and blood but against the rulers, against the authorities, against the powers of this dark world and against the spiritual forces of evil in the heavenly realms*" (Ephesians 6:12).

The fourth chapter of Luke tells the story of Jesus, our perfect example, full of the Holy Spirit being led by the Spirit into the wilderness. There Satan tempted Him for 40 days. Verse 13 says, "*When the devil had finished all this tempting, he left Him until an opportune time.*"

Satan continued his testing throughout Jesus' life and ministry. Satan will continue to test us throughout our life and ministry, as well. The book of Nehemiah is a wonderful study in how to fulfill a God-given task while experiencing and overcoming opposition. Following are helpful principles taken from the life of the prophet Nehemiah:

1. Expect opposition when doing the will of God.
2. Pray! Become a woman of prayer. Nehemiah led on his knees.
3. Fast! Seek God for His timing, direction, vision, etc.
4. Always exercise discretion. Be slow to speak.
5. Say only what God says, not what the enemy says.
6. Realize the importance of strategy and assessment before taking action.

7. When angry, don't immediately react. Pray and then confront others when calm and with measured words.

8. Don't make light of serious offense.

9. Campaign for the right things with authority, always remembering who you are and Whose you are.

10. Nehemiah lived what he taught. Therefore he taught with authority and humility, not in pride. We can too!

11. Remember that one pastors' wife can make a difference.

I pray that these principles encourage you as you continue to fight the good fight of faith.

"Sure I must fight, if I would reign; increase my courage, Lord; I'll bear the toil, endure the pain, Supported by thy word."[13]

28

The Making of a Mentor

Within the span of one month a few different doctors told me a few different changes in my body were "normal, considering my age." The crowning blow came during my daily morning ritual of lightly rubbing moisturizing cream (heavily laced with glycolic acid and sunscreen) on my face. What I thought was a runaway streak of the white cream turned out to be a hair—firmly rooted to my scalp. Although I feel great, exercise regularly, eat right, and can still do cartwheels, it's as if my body is part of some covert conspiracy I know nothing about and betrays me continually.

Almost simultaneous with the physical changes I'm experiencing, a few young women have asked me if I would prayerfully consider "mothering" or mentoring them. The timing of their requests reminded me that another normal occurrence within a maturing Body is the living out of

Titus 2:3-5. *"Likewise, teach the older women to be reverent in the way they live, not to be slanderers or addicted to much wine, but to teach what is good. Then they can train the younger women to love their husbands and children, to be self-controlled and pure, to be busy at home, to be kind, and to be subject to their husbands, so that no one will malign the word of God."*

Pastors' wives are in a prime position to positively affect the women in their churches, both young and old. All Christians are Christ's representatives. However as pastors' wives we tend to receive more careful scrutiny than the average woman in the church. That fact challenges me to make my life worth watching and imitating. For some, the thought of scrutiny and imitation makes them want to run for cover. That's how it used to make me feel. Now it serves as a tool that helps teach me to live a life that glorifies God and blesses others.

In the book *Help! I'm A Pastor's Wife*, Devi Titus writes, *"As the pastor's wife, I am set up to be an example to the flock. The definition of "example" is "to act in such a way as to arouse the imitation of others." How can people imitate me unless they watch me and evaluate me? Recognizing this basic principle of discipleship helped to change my attitude toward the scrutiny I receive. It has also enforced a discipline in my life that I would probably not have had otherwise."*[14]

In the secular arena, confidence, higher education, success in one's career, and ascending the proverbial corporate ladder, may be qualities needed to mentor others. Pastors' wives, however, who display an exemplary measure of spiritual maturity are poised to be a blessing to those precious younger women God places in their congregations.

Although there are many ways to mentor, I've listed a few essentials that make for a successful mentoring relationship.

- **A**gree on an objective.

What does the person hope to gain from such a relationship? Are their expectations realistic? If so, are you able to meet them? However flattered you may feel in being asked to mentor, there may be another woman who is better suited for the task. Remember, *"Pride goes before destruction, a haughty spirit before a fall"* (Proverbs 16:18).

- **B**uild a relationship.

It's hard to speak into someone's life when you don't really know one another. Although the objective of your mentoring relationship is not friendship, be open to the possibility. Become acquainted with your mentee's hobbies, interests, job, birthday, etc. Loving, thoughtful acts of kindness show you care.

- **C**ommit to an agreed upon length of time for getting together and how often. (This may need adjusting.)

- **D**iscuss and define terms, such as accountability.

It is not uncommon for mentees to resent the mothering they've asked for, especially when they want to "do their own thing." This is where the love, wisdom, and commitment of the mentor are invaluable. *"As iron sharpens iron, so one man sharpens [develops and molds his character] another"* (Proverbs 27:17).

- **E**ncourage

"Do not let unwholesome talk come out of your mouth, but only what is helpful for building others up according to their needs, that it may benefit those who listen" (Ephesians 4:29).

- **F**ollow the Leader

Remember, we are not out to make clones of ourselves, but to model Christ in such a way that the mentee(s) becomes more like Him. *"Follow my example, as I follow the example of Christ"* (1 Corinthians 1:11).

29

Who Mentors the Mentor?

E very pastor's wife can benefit from having a role model or mentor. So when God pointed out a particular woman and said that I could learn a lot from her, I sought to become better acquainted with a woman with whom I was only fairly familiar. Actually, I knew her husband and son far better but had never really spent time getting to know the woman within this beautiful wife and loving mother.

What little I did know of her hardly seemed to qualify one as a model mentor. She was known for telling half-truths (and growing up I was told a half-truth is bad as a whole lie). Sometimes she took submission to her husband to levels of co-dependency. Once, she let her big mouth get her into big trouble and later blamed it all on her husband. And probably worst of all, it was common knowledge that in her anger, frustration, and without apology, she had a young mother and son evicted and thrown out in the street.

Lest I be guilty of gossiping, this is all thankfully in the past. She is now a shining example of God's amazing grace and the unfading inner beauty that radiates from a life of faith. I'd now like to share with you what I'm learning from Sarah, the wife of Abraham and mother of Isaac.

The call upon your husband's life is a call upon your life. I've struggled to maintain a firm grasp on this. So did Sarah. God appeared to her husband and said, *"Leave your country, your people and your father's household and go to the land I will show you. I will make you into a great nation and I will bless you, and whoever curses you I will curse; and all peoples on earth will be blessed through you"* (Genesis 12:2-3). God told this to Abraham several different times (see Genesis 13:14-17, 15:4-5, 17:1-14).

While Sarah accompanied Abraham, there is no mentioning of where or how she figured into this divine proclamation. Pastors' wives often feel this way. God called my husband but what about me? It's not until four chapters and many event-full years later that Sarah's name is mentioned in direct relation to God's call upon Abraham's life. During those years, Sarah suffered several significant identity crises.

You must know who you are. Many pastors' wives can get confused with roles versus reality, personal identity and people's perceptions. Sarah also struggled. At times she carried herself as Abraham's wife. At other times she said she was his sister. As evidenced by Sarah's life, failure to know and see yourself within your husband's calling can misplace others and lead to disgrace (Hagar and Ishmael, Genesis 16 & 21:9-20).

Sarah also suffered separation from Abraham while living a double life. Unless we are true to ourselves—knowing who we are, Whose we are, and staying true to both, we cannot be true to others. *"Fear of man will prove to be a snare, but whoever trusts in the Lord is kept safe"* (Proverbs 29:25).

God may speak to your husband about you. *"God also said to Abraham, "As for Sarai your wife, you are no longer to call her Sarai; her name will be Sarah. I will bless her and will surely give you a son by her. I will bless her so that she will be the mother of nations; kings of peoples will come from her"* (Genesis 17:15-16).

Notice that God is speaking to Abraham about Sarah. God knows who you are and what He wants to accomplish through you. Precious pastor's wife, God can be trusted to speak to your husband...even when doubt arises. *"Abraham fell facedown; he laughed and said to himself, "Will a son be born to a man a hundred years old? Will Sarah bear a child at the age of ninety?" Then God said, "Yes...your wife Sarah will bear you a son and you will call him Isaac...I will establish my covenant with him as an everlasting covenant for his descendants after him...whom Sarah will bear to you by this time next year"* (Genesis 17:17-19, 21).

Trust God to make His will known to you. In Genesis 18:1-15 we read the account of God, once again, speaking to Abraham. This time, however, Sarah is present and listening. Ladies, God is fully aware of you. He hears your heart, and knows each anxious thought. *"Is there anything too hard for the Lord"* (Genesis 18:14)? Are *you* listening?

Learn to laugh—when, how, and why. When God revealed His wonderful will to Sarah, she laughed to herself and thought, *"After I am worn out and my master is old, will I now have this pleasure"* (Genesis 18:12)? Don't doubt and laugh off God's promises to you. Becoming a woman of faith requires focusing on the promises not the problems.

After the birth of Isaac, which incidentally means—to laugh, Sarah has cause to rejoice and laugh for joy. *"Sarah said, "God has brought me laughter, and everyone who hears about this will laugh with me." And she added, "Who would have said to Abraham that Sarah would nurse children? Yet I have borne him a son in his old age"* (Genesis 21:6-7).

Like mother, like daughter. Sarah learned to trust God and her husband. *"You are her daughters if you do what is right and do not give way to fear"* (1 Peter 3:6).

30

Growing Pains

B efore Paul and I married, many of our dates consisted of going to some church where he was invited to preach. Therefore, after marrying I was already used to accompanying him on preaching assignments. What I was not accustomed to was serving with him. I was his travel companion, cheerleader, and personal valet. I proudly pressed and starched his shirts. I made sure that he had his Bible and notes. I kept handkerchiefs, business cards, toiletries, and extra changes of clothing ready, like a well-stocked "Pastor's First Aid Kit." I made sure never to be without a ready smile, warm embrace, listening ear, and a shoulder to cry on. I thought that was all it took to be a good pastor's wife. How wrong I was.

After a funeral service that my husband officiated, I went home in tears realizing that my idea of ministry was being challenged. I went along with him and sat towards the back. My dislike of funerals was so great that I even grew to hate the smell of fresh flowers.

This gathering was small, intimate, just the family and a few acquaintances. I felt out of place. Witnessing their grief seemed like an invasion of privacy. Afterwards as those assembled made ready to go to the cemetery, it became apparent that there were more floral arrangements than the funeral director and his assistant could quickly carry to the hearse. Someone asked if I would be going to the graveside and thrust a large basket of flowers into my arms when they heard me say, "Yes." But I was only riding with the minister. I wasn't getting out of the car. Without asking my permission, I was told to help carry the flowers.

My sudden tears had nothing to do with the family's loss. I wept because I felt scared and selfish, because I was carrying funeral flowers, because I was going to the cemetery and getting out of the car, because I was doing something I had not foreseen. That night I wrote in my journal, *"Lord, I didn't bargain for this aspect of Paul's ministry..."*

Somehow I only saw ministry as what my husband did, not me. How naïve and shortsighted I was. I poured out my thoughts, fears, and apprehensions onto the pages of my journal and in prayer. I wrote and wrestled. And in the end, I surrendered.

"I didn't bargain for this aspect of Paul's ministry, but I surrender to it. I am involved in ministry because we are saved to serve. Father, I surrender to this call

*to ministry upon my life, not just my husband's. You
know just how many different ways I'm not even close
to being ready for service, nevertheless I surrender to
it. Prepare me, day by day. Yes, to Your will. Yes,
unconditionally yes!"*

Like many pastors' wives, I used to be fearful of so many things. I believe that is why so many women married to pastors dislike the ministry. We are more aware of our weaknesses than we are of God's grace.

The Greek word for grace is charis, meaning calmly happy due to God's divine influence upon one's heart, and its reflection in the life. Grace is a supernatural enabling or ability from God, to do what pleases Him.

Scripture says, *"...apart from me you can do nothing"* (John 15:5). However, in Philippians 4:13 we read, "*I can do everything through him who gives me strength.*" Simply put, grace is God's power that comes to help His children in their weakness!

It is amazing to see what God will do with and through a life that is surrendered to Him. My transformation did not happen overnight. It's gradual, ongoing, day-by-day and moment-to-moment. Many times in prayer I use the very words Jesus prayed in the Garden of Gethsemane, *"Nevertheless, not my will but thine be done."*

In the book *Who Is The Minister's Wife*, Charlotte Ross writes, *"It was an act of love that called forth the giving of herself in marriage. It is an act of love that calls forth the giving of herself in ministry. The clergy wife is one who, for the love of a man—her husband—is a partner in love with the GOD/ MAN—her Lord Jesus. The giving of herself in ministry is a cherished gift to be held in honor and it will be used by the Lord Jesus."*[15]

The journal entry I shared was written over 30 years ago. I thought about it recently while flying cross-country to attend a funeral. The mother of one of our members passed away. I would be representing my husband and church, and giving condolences during the service. It was the third such trip I'd made in a year.

Whatever you face that you would rather run away from, God says to you, "My grace is sufficient for you, for my power is made perfect in weakness."

As you surrender may you respond like the apostle Paul, *"Therefore I will boast all the more gladly about my weaknesses so that Christ's power may rest on me. That is why, for Christ's sake, I delight in weaknesses, in insults, in hardships, in persecutions in difficulties. For when I am weak, then I am strong"* (2 Corinthians 12:9-10).

31

Pleasing God

When I was in elementary school we read lots of Aesop's fables. These stories taught such life skills as compassion, effort, honesty, patience, perseverance, problem solving, responsibility, teamwork, and wisdom. One of the fables I particularly liked was The Man, His Son, and Their Donkey. Following is my updated version of that story.

> *A man and his son were taking their donkey to sell in a nearby town. Before long they met a group of teenagers. One said, "Look at those two fools walking when they could be riding." So the man put his son on the donkey's back and they continued on their way.*
>
> *Next they came upon a group of senior citizens. One of the old men said, "Young people today just don't respect their elders. Look at that disrespectful boy riding while his poor old father walks. Young man,*

you ought to be ashamed of yourself!" The father made his son dismount and got on the donkey's back in his place.

Further on in their journey they passed by a group of women and children. "Look at that case of child abuse," the women cried! "How can you ride while your little boy walks. He can hardly keep up with you. You could be reported to Child Protective Services!" The man, wishing to please, lifted the boy up behind him.

Just as they reached the edge of town an animal rights activist shouted, "I ought to report you to the Humane Society for overloading that poor animal. You big, lazy men could carry the donkey better than he carries you." So the man and his son got off and carried the donkey over the bridge that led to the next town. People came running from all over to look and laugh at the strange sight. The poor donkey, frightened by the uproar, began struggling to get down. In the midst of the confusion the donkey slipped, fell off the bridge, and drowned.

Moral: When you try to please all, you please none.

As a pastor's wife who has often struggled with getting and keeping the donkey off of my back, this story is more relevant to me now than when I was a little girl. The actions of many pastors' wives are often dictated by a desire to please others and do what's expected of us. The moral to that story is: When you try to please all, you end up displeasing God.

We need to know that we honor God best as we serve Him by using the gifts and personality He has given us. We were created to experience fulfillment as we discover and use our gifts for the work God called us to do, thus bringing Him glory. As we use our gifts, the Holy Spirit enables us to serve and please God with authority, boldness, and confidence.

The following seven keys will help you discover and exercise your spiritual gifts.

1. **Ask**: The same Holy Spirit who gives the gifts will reveal them to us as we seek His guidance and help (Matthew 7:7-11, John 16:13, James 1:5).

2. **Burdens**: Nehemiah's burden to rebuild the wall of Jerusalem was an indication that the hand of God was upon him to perform that task (Nehemiah 1:1-11). Therefore, identify those needs that especially trouble you and find out which gift(s) meet those needs.

3. **Conferral**: Some gifts are imparted by prophecy or the laying on of hands (1 Timothy 1:18, 4:14, 2 Timothy 1:6). Unless this is confirmation of what the Lord has already revealed to you, always ask the Holy Spirit to confirm the validity of what others have spoken to you.

4. **Dreams**: When our motives are pure, the dreams, visions, and deep desires we have often indicate God's will for our lives (Joel 2:28, Psalm 37:4). Find out which gift(s) will enable you to fulfill your God-given dream.

5. **Exposure**: Some things are caught rather than taught (2 Kings 2:9-13, 2 Timothy 1:5-6). Expose yourself to people who are already exercising their gifts.

6. **Faith**: Since you know that God wants to use you, exercise faith by dismissing from your mind all excuses, delays, and limitations (Hebrews 11:1, 6). Feed your faith and starve your doubts!

7. **Go for it!** Faith without works is dead (James 2:15-17). Genuine faith must be accompanied by action. We must act in faith, not fear, when given the opportunity to use our gifts.

32

So Long Superwoman

Admittedly I write about Mary and Martha quite a bit. That's because I tend to be a Martha—too stressed to be blessed, longing to be a Mary—too blessed to be stressed (see Luke 10:38-42).

Without benefit of a red cape, blue tights, and a large S on my chest, I fly through my days like Superwoman. Living this way is incredibly exhausting. My outer life begins to resemble my disorganized and distracted inner life. Freshly laundered clothes sit wrinkling in baskets. Tax papers are in too many places. A growing pile of unopened mail threatens to topple over. The carpets are clean but the vacuum still stands in the corner. If I were a little girl that's where I would be standing for failing to complete my assignments.

What started all this? While seeking fulfillment, little by little I began over-committing. Saying, "I'll do it," is easy. There's that initial excitement that accompanies accepting responsibility for an assigned task. However, a beginning blaze of enthusiasm can fizzle to a flicker for lack of follow through. A misguided search for satisfaction led to my taking on the unassigned, which eventually became the unfinished.

Sadly, I've been in this place before. Busyness becomes a bolster whenever my self-esteem is lagging or when I confuse "doing" with "being." At those times instead of spending quality time in God's presence and speaking to myself in psalms, hymns, and spiritual songs, I talk myself into taking on too much.

The sight and thought of unfinished tasks either spurs me into a frenzy of agitated activity or immobilizes me. I'm either busy playing catch-up or wandering around in a daze wondering where do I begin? Both leave me completely tired and frustrated.

It's hard staying out of the performance pit. Pastors' wives may be particularly vulnerable to falling in this area. Succumbing to the pressures of unrealistic expectations (our own and those of others), good intentions, or a lack of contentment makes slipping back in a constant threat. It can happen when we lose sight of who we are in Christ, seeking to do that for which we are not gifted, or having impure motives.

God is all for us living lives of passion and purpose. He came that we might have life and have it to the full (John 10:10). However if we seek passion and purpose outside of Him, our search is in vain, even if what we're doing *seems* godly.

First Timothy 6:6 says, *"Godliness with contentment is great gain"* or as I heard one Bible teacher say, "Your attitude determines your altitude." It's hard to lift up the Lord when you're down in the dumps.

For quite some time busyness masked my discontent. But "doing" failed to fill the void within. In some ways it only served to exacerbate the emptiness. What was once a delight became duty and drudgery. Living and looking at life from a very low altitude made my daily routine seem more like a rut. Without gladness, even serving the Lord can feel futile. His joy is our strength. Working in one's own strength guarantees fatigue and burnout. Personal strength has its limits. When human strength gives out it is only a matter of time before we give up.

Contentment is the state of being satisfied with what one is or has, not wanting more or anything else, and ease of mind. The passage in 1 Timothy 6:6 seems to suggest that it is entirely possible to do good even godly things without contentment. Before long that lack of contentment takes away from the good one does. Without contentment, serving begins to feel like slavery. Far more often than I care to admit, my busyness mirrors that of Martha (Luke 10:38-42).

Martha, although obviously hospitable, became cumbered, overloaded, burdened, troubled, and inconvenienced

132

by her serving. She insinuates that Jesus does not care about all her hard work in His behalf and that her sister Mary is lazy. Even in her agitation Martha does the right thing by taking her burdens to the Lord. In verses 41 and 42 Jesus clearly demonstrates His awareness of Martha's predicament and tells her how to remedy the problem. Jesus does not tell Martha to stop what she is doing nor does He tell Mary to help her. Rather He points out the fact that Mary has chosen contentment—satisfaction, ease of mine about who she is, what she has, what she is doing—and that will not be taken away from her.

Sisters, contentment is a choice holding the promise of great gain. By choosing contentment we can stop striving to be Superwoman and live joyfully as supernaturally blessed women.

33

Faith's Lamplighters

When I was eight years old my mother gave me the gift of Robert Louis Stevenson's book, A Child's Garden Of Verses. One of the many poems I still enjoy is The Lamplighter. It tells of a young boy's fascination with Leerie, the town's lamplighter. Leerie walks the darkening streets with ladder and lantern stopping to light the streetlamps, including one that is just outside the youngster's window. In one verse the little boy, the son of a rich banker, tells of the careers he and his siblings will pursue when they grow up. His brother Tom desires to be a driver while sister Maria dreams of adventure and sailing the high seas. This little lad, however, wants to grow strong and go around at night lighting lamps with Leerie.

I thought of that poem while attending a retreat for pastors' wives. Also in attendance were such luminaries as Vonette Bright, Lynne Dugan, and Ann Ortlund. These are just a few of the women God has used to bear the light and hope of the glorious gospel. They have illumined lives while bringing the light and love of Christ to a cold and dark world. These women were my first role models, my Leeries.

During the early days of my husband's pastorate when I felt completely in the dark about being a pastor's wife, God used their books and ministries to shed light on my many questions and concerns. Till death, they faithfully bore the flame—carrying the torch for Christ, enlightening hearts, minds, and lives.

They started running the Christian race many years ago. Bearing the message of the Messiah they proclaimed the good news of both abundant and eternal life. They relayed hope for the brokenhearted, and the freedom from bondage that threatens to imprison and prevent others from experiencing and enjoying their inheritance in Christ.

Scripture exhorts older women who have themselves been taught, to teach or to train younger women. The Greek verb translated "train" means to discipline, to moderate, to make sane or sober of mind. This is similar to what a coach does for athletes. The coach is one who instructs, drills, and prepares others. Coaches help others to learn.

"Likewise, teach the older women to be reverent in the way they live, not to be slanderers or addicted to much wine, but to teach what is good. Then they can train the younger women to love their husbands and children, to be self-controlled and pure, to be busy

at home, to be kind, and to be subject to their hus-
bands, so that no one will malign the word of God"
(Titus 2:3-5).

Over thirty-seven years ago as a young pastor's wife, I looked for spiritually mature women to speak into my life— those who could agitate, stir up, and fan into flame all that smoldered within me. Today we often call this passing down of knowledge and training from one who is more experienced to another who is less experienced, mentoring. A mentor encourages and equips another for excellence.

Just like the little boy in Stevenson's poem, countless new and young ministry wives look for those who will come along with ladder and lantern to scale what can appear to be insurmountable situations in life and shed light on the insecurity and doubt that can dim one's faith. We can become those women—God's faithful messengers who bear His image, His light, and His love and then share it with others.

It only takes a spark to get a fire going,
And soon all those around can warm up to its glowing.
That's how it is with God's love,
Once you've experienced it, you spread His love to everyone,
You want to pass it on.[16]

Jesus is the
Reason For
the Season

34

The Gift That Keeps On Giving

For two Christmases back-to-back I forgot a gift. Both times the gifts were carefully selected with the recipient in mind and lovingly purchased. One year the forgotten gift was a CD for our son. On Christmas morning, in the merriment of giving and exchanging gifts, I was completely unaware that any were missing. Later that evening Aaron mentioned the CD. What followed was a frantic search, lasting almost a month. Finally the forgotten gift was found. Amid the hustle and bustle of the holidays, beneath the gaily colored wrappings and trappings of Christmas, the CD was simply overlooked and then forgotten.

The next Christmas was pretty much the same. Again there was the usual excited hustle and bustle. The holidays create quite a stir that, if not watched carefully, can lead to overwhelming frustration and the kind of kind of busyness that Martha experienced (Luke 10:38-42 NIV). Much like Martha, I too opened my home and almost immediately became *"distracted by all the preparations that had to be made."*

The word distracted is cumbered in the KJV Bible and means: to drag one's care and circumstances all around; troubled about many things; to take a person's mind off what he or she is doing; distraught.

It hardly seems possible but somehow buried beneath cumbersome cares and circumstances, I forgot the Greatest Gift—Jesus Christ the reason for the season. And like Martha, the Lord had to say to me, "You are worried and upset about many things, but only one thing is needed."

The time spent looking for the forgotten CD pales in comparison to the forfeiture of peace and the needless pain experienced by forgetting Jesus Christ. What I needed most from my heavenly Father was lovingly purchased and freely given, but I forgot this most precious Gift. However, the joy in finding my Gift is beyond compare.

Perhaps you, too, overlooked your Gift. Maybe you are worried and upset about many things. Only one thing is needed—sitting at Jesus' feet and listening to what He says. When we turn our hearts to the Lord, He pours out His heart to us and makes His thoughts known to us. (Proverbs 1:23)

"Ask and it will be given to you; seek and you will find; knock and the door will be opened to you. For everyone who asks receives; he who seeks finds; and to him who knocks, the door will be opened.

If you, then, though you are evil, know how to give good gifts to your children, how much more will your Father in heaven give good gifts to those who ask him"

(Matthew 7:7-8, 11)!

"Jesus Christ is the same yesterday and today and forever (Hebrews 13:8)." He is the reason for the season and the Gift that keeps on giving, long after the holidays have passed. He is:

Author and Finisher of our faith

Burden Bearer

Comforter, Counselor

Defender, Deliverer

Emmanuel

Friend

God's Greatest Gift and Giver of every good and

perfect gift

Healer, Helper

Intercessor

Jehovah-Jireh: God our provider

King of Kings

Lifter of our heads, Lover of our souls

Master, Maker

Name above all names

Overseer

Prince of Peace

Quieting the storms of life

Refiner, Revealer, Our Righteousness

Savior

Truth

Upholding the righteous

Our Victory

The living Word and Water

Our perfect eXample

Yokemate

Zealously in love with you!

Enjoy your Gift!

35

Let Every Heart Prepare Him Room

P roblem people—we all know some. Every church has
them. Sometimes, they've stared at us from our mirrors. Certainly, places of employment, churches, neighbor-
hoods, and life in general, would be better without them.
Or would they?

While reading the gospel of John, I was struck by the
procession of problem people found parading through Jesus'
life. There were those who persecuted and sought to kill Him
because of His miracle working power. Others murmured
and complained about His prophetic preaching. Some who
once followed, later rejected His teachings and turned their
backs on the Word made flesh. The religious authorities
rejected Him. One of His disciples betrayed Him.

What possible purpose do problem people serve? Psalm 119:71 may hold the answer.

"It was good for me to be afflicted so that I might learn your decrees."

It's hard to learn God's decrees when preoccupied with wanting to teach someone a lesson. During a scene from an old western movie, a man who's had one too many encounters with a problem person seeks to take matters into his own hands. The country preacher tries reasoning with the man and says, "You know, the Good Book says, "Vengeance is mine," saith the Lord." To which the man replies, "I don't have a problem with that, as long as He doesn't take too long and I can watch."

We've all been tempted to take matters into our own hands or relished the idea of seeing someone get their just due. No matter how often I read the book of John, a tiny part of me wishes that there was a record of Jesus at least setting Judas straight. Judas, a disciple chosen by Christ and who later would betray Him, served as the treasurer even though he was a thief (John 12:6). Why then isn't there an account of Jesus saying, "Look Judas, I've had about enough of you. These here are The 12 disciples, not The Dirty Dozen. Get out!"

Jesus, the sinless Son of God, learned obedience through the things He suffered. When afflicted, He demonstrated love and forgiveness. The goal then is not to destroy or devalue problem people, but if at all possible, to make disciples of them.

> *"A new command I give you: Love one another. As I have loved you, so you must love one another. By this all men will know that you are my disciples, if you love one another"* (John 13:34-35).

Here, and in several other passages in this book, Jesus exhorts us to love one another. It is a command, not a suggestion. We are commanded by God to love those who cheer us on and those who criticize our best efforts. Our love must be without partiality; extended to both the lovely and unlovely, the wonderful ones and the ones we wonder about.

Christmas is a time to share warm and fuzzy holiday greetings. But sometimes, that's when we need a word of encouragement from the Lord to help us face the New Year. God knows the heartache you feel when your pastor/husband comes under attack by those within the congregation or on church boards or staff. The Lord knows those of you whose hearts are heavy due to problem people in your congregation, on your jobs, in your families, and in the world. He also sees those who feel insecure, devalued, unaccepted, unloved and without purpose—those who in their sin or brokenness become problem people. He is the solution for all. *"For God so loved the world that he gave his one and only Son...* (John 3:16)."

This holiday season, may you rejoice afresh in the glorious gifts that God has given you: His Son, His Spirit, His peace, His power, and His love. As you trim your Christmas trees may you remember that Jesus hung on a tree that all who believe in Him may have abundant and eternal life. As you string lights, may you remember that we are called to be the light of the world. And by the transforming love of Christ, may problem people find room in your hearts.

36

Remembering God's Greatest Gift

I t's hard to believe that another year is coming to an end. But isn't it wonderful that as the year ends we celebrate with a season of gift giving in remembrance of the greatest Gift ever given?!

John 3:16 says, *"For God so loved the world that he gave his one and only Son, that whoever believes in him shall not perish but have everlasting life."*

Yes, we end the year remembering and reveling in God's amazing love—the gift of His Son, Jesus Christ. *"For to us a child is born, to us a son is given, and the government will be on his shoulders. And he will be called Wonderful Counselor, Mighty God, Everlasting Father, Prince of Peace"* (Isaiah 9:6).

God has impeccable taste and spares no expense giving great gifts. *"Every good and perfect gift is from above, coming down from the Father of the heavenly lights, who does not change like shifting shadows"* (James 1:17).

The word good in this passage means: of good constitution or nature, useful, pleasant, agreeable, joyful, happy, excellent, distinguished, honorable, and upright.

Perfect means: brought to its end, finished, wanting nothing necessary to completeness. There is no lack in what God gives!

Another of His good gifts is you! That's right. Proverbs 18:22 says, *"He who finds a wife finds what is good and receives favor from the LORD."* You are "God's gift" to your husband. Without you, your husband would be lacking. With you he is blessed, benefitted, and receives favor from the Lord.

Pastors' wives need to know how very much God loves you. God values you. You are precious to Him and hold an important place in the body of Christ—standing beside the man of God, another of His gifts.

"I will give you shepherds after my own heart, who will lead you with knowledge and understanding" (Jeremiah 3:15).

Your husband may be the more visible and vocal partner, but God sees you as well. As a matter of fact, He can't take His eyes off of you. *"The eyes of the Lord are on the righteous and his ears are open to their cry"* (Psalm 34:15).

"The eyes of the Lord are everywhere, keeping watch on the evil and the good" (Proverbs 15:3).

"For the eyes of the Lord are on the righteous and his ears are attentive to their prayers..." (1 Peter 3:12).

If you're still not convinced of your worth and value, then look in the mirror. James 1:22-25 MSG says, *"Don't fool yourself into thinking that you are a listener when you are anything but, letting the Word go in one ear and out the other. Act on what you hear! Those who hear and don't act are like those who glance in the mirror, walk away, and two minutes later have no idea who they are, what they look like. But whoever catches a glimpse of the revealed counsel of God—the free life—even out of the corner of his eye, and sticks with it, is no distracted scatterbrain but a man or woman of action. That person will find delight and affirmation on the action."*

This Christmas season as we give and receive gifts, let us remember and rejoice in Jesus—God's greatest gift! And then remember that you are a gift. You are good, valuable, precious, and being perfected!

37

Sweet Endings

T his recipe is a Christmas morning tradition in our
home. I love having my family awaken to the smell of
Monkey Bread wafting through the house. I put it together
the night before and bake it on Christmas morning. It's
super simple and simply delicious! Here's the recipe. Enjoy!

About 20 frozen Rhodes Bake-N-Serve dinner rolls

1 (3 ounce) package of butterscotch Cook-and-Serve
   pudding mix (not instant)

3/4 cup of brown sugar, packed

1 teaspoon of cinnamon

1/2 cup of chopped pecans

1/2 cup (1 stick) of unsalted butter, melted

Instructions

The night before you want to serve these rolls, thoroughly
butter or spray a Bundt pan and place the frozen dinner rolls
in the bottom. Sprinkle with the powdered pudding mix.

Mix together the brown sugar and cinnamon and sprinkle on top of the frozen rolls. Sprinkle top with the pecans and pour melted butter all over the top. Cover loosely with plastic wrap and let rise in a draft free place, for about 7 hours, or overnight. (I put mine in an unheated oven or microwave.)

When ready to bake, remove the risen rolls from the oven (if that's where you put yours). Preheat oven to 350 degrees and bake for about 25 to 30 minutes. Loosen around the edges of the pan and the center tube and let rest a few minutes; turn out onto a large plate. Let cool slightly and serve warm.

About the Author

As a pastor's wife since 1982, Meredith has a keen understanding of the unique challenges faced by ministry wives. Her desire to connect with fellow pastors' wives is rooted in her belief that we are stronger as a sisterhood and need each other's camaraderie and support.

Through Wives In Touch, a ministry of prayer and encouragement for pastors' wives, she shares both her life experiences and solid biblical hope for women in the trenches of serving the body of Christ. The WIT newsletter offers hope, encouragement, and practical advice for PWs throughout the United States and abroad.

In addition to WIT, Meredith has served on the Advisory Board of the First Lady Conference hosted by Dr. Lois Evans, the Urban Alternative of Dallas, Texas (2000 – 2011), and on the advisory team of the Global Pastors' Wives Network (GPWN). Meredith has also shared her message of encouragement through the ministries of Excellent Living and Just Between Us.

A true lover of words, Meredith enjoys reading, journaling, and playing Scrabble. If any of these can be done while on a cruise, well, that's even better. Meredith and her husband Paul have two grown children, Alicia and Aaron, and a black lab named Zoey.

38

Endnotes

Chapter 1: The Journey Begins
1   Somebody Somewhere Is Prayin' (Just For You) by Andrae Crouch 1984 Word Entertainment

Chapter 2: Leaving, Lodging, and Loving
2   All The Women In The Bible by Sue and Larry Richards, Thomas Nelson Publishing; Everything In The Bible Series edition (May 31, 1999)
3   Hymn Where He Leads Me written by E.W. Blandy, Copyright Public Domain

Chapter 3: Basic Training
4   Heart To Heart With Pastors' Wives © Copyright 1994 by Lynne Dugan, Published by Regal Books a division of Gospel Light National Association of Evangelicals (NAE): 1023 15th Street, N.W., Suite 500, Washington, DC 20005 (202-789-1011)
5   High Call, High Privilege © Copyright 1988 by Gail MacDonald, Published by Hendrickson Publishers, Inc., E. Stanley Jones, The Way (Nashville: Abingdon, 1946), p. 197

Chapter 4: Designer's Original
6   The Private Life of the Minister's Wife by Betty J. Coble, Broadman Press (1981)
7   Designer's Original by Danniebelle Hall, A&M (1982)

Chapter 14: Dealing With Betrayal
8   Webster's New World Dictionary, Houghton Mifflin (2012)

9   The Wounded Heart by Dr. Dan Allender, NavPress

Chapter 17: Reach Out and Touch Someone

10 Help! I'm a Pastor's Wife, Edited by Michele Buckingham, Creation House, Strang Communications, © Copyright 1986, Excerpt from chapter 32 – Supporting One Another by Jean Coleman

Chapter 19: Relationships

11 The Friendships of Women by Dee Brestin, David C. Cook; New edition (July 1, 2008)

12 Can I Afford Time For Friendships by Stormie Omartian, Ruth Senter, Colleen Evans, Bethany House Publishers, © Copyright 1994

Chapter 27: Fighting the Good Fight of Faith

13 Am I a Soldier of the Cross? by Isaac Watts, pub.ca 1721, Public Domain

Chapter 28: The Making of a Mentor

14 Help! I'm a Pastor's Wife, Charisma Media (June 1, 1986)

Chapter 30: Growing Pains

15 Who Is the Minister's Wife?: A Search for Personal Fulfillment, Charlotte Ross, Westminster John Knox Press

Chapter 33: Faith's Lamplighters

16   Song: Pass It On by Kurt Kaiser, © Copyright 1969 Bud John Songs (Admin. EMI Christian Music Publishing)

CPSIA information can be obtained
at www.ICGtesting.com
Printed in the USA
FSHW020057220921